the Pendulum of Choice

Cover Design by Joe Lee

the Pendulum of Choice

by JOHANNA ALEMANN

Maxim Publishing

ISBN: 0—936696—00—1

Library of Congress Catalogue Number: 80—81252

Copyright © 1980 by Johanna Alemann

FIRST EDITION: June 1980

Published by:

Maxim Publishing
P. O. Box 42126
Los Angeles, California 90042

Printed in the United States of America

TABLE OF CONTENTS

THE PENDULUM OF CHOICE
is written for growth people who seek
comfort and security in their inner worlds
as a resolution to life's predicaments.

ACKNOWLEDGEMENTS

Every author is fortunate enough to draw upon the generous help from knowledgeable well-wishers, and I have incorporated many excellent suggestions for which I am deeply grateful. I wish to especially thank

SIDONIE FLACCO, M.ED., MFCC,

an inspired marriage and family counselor in California, for her contributions to and validation of the self-help concepts presented. She developed the rudiments of her counseling ethics while supervising innovative community projects. She is a sought-after counselor, equally accomplished in conducting private therapy sessions or growth workshops for groups.

We proceeded from the optimistic viewpoint that any negative attitude or habit pattern can be transformed into a positive learning experience, helping the self-improvers in their quest to become wholesome, lovable and thereby happy. It was our mutual aim to present goals and solutions that are entirely attainable, having proved valid in Sidonie Flacco's years of service and dedication. I am most grateful for the generous sharing of her professional counseling methods.

FOREWORD

The pendulum of opposites swings in constant motion throughout our lives. It jolts us to the brink of desperation, leaves us exhilarated when we are moved to ecstasy, and agitates us into action when we are complacent.

If we allow the pendulum to drive us from one opposite to the other, our emotions sway in a continuous state of upheaval. As we learn to stay within the comfort zone of our inner climate, we replace the undesirable with the desirable. In the times of balance and integration, a perfect feeling of harmony is experienced.

Understanding duality gives us the clue to master our life from youth to old age. We can avoid the pitfalls that lurk on the negative end of extremes and opt for positive choices. They are loving, building and purposeful. We cannot stop the swing of the pendulum nor can we escape its motion, but we can regulate it, so we may lead a joyful existence and feel at home in the world.

THE QUESTIONNAIRES:
A SPECIAL FEATURE

Dear Reader: You will find a set of questions or statements interwoven into the various concepts presented in this book, such as:

☐   Why did I experience a sudden mood swing?

☐   Why did I act against my better judgment?

☐   What was the cause of my personality change?

You might wish to review your intentions, while contemplating the duality of your life. This feature scrves the following purposes:

*   To summarize key ideas;

*   To interweave guidelines, healing dynamics,
      and problem-solving solutions;

*   To get you in touch with your personal needs;

*   To help you discover your priorities.

☐ Boxes are provided that you may check concepts which are relevant to you. I hope you will utilize this feature as a memory aid. From time to time you may wish to check on your progress... or renew good intentions... or simply reinforce the values and aspirations that you consider important to your future.

INTRODUCTION

THE PENDULUM OF DUALITY

Have you not noticed that the
end of each thought
reveals its opposite?
(Henrik Ibsen)

I cannot master my life
without understanding the
forces of duality.

According to the laws of duality
day supersedes night
and reason defeats doom.
(Jacob Boehme)

THE FORCES OF DUALITY

Sooner or later there comes a time when we realize that we cannot have everything that we desire. Dreams may not materialize, there are limits to our expectations and success cannot be requisitioned. If our ambitions deserve praise, why do they falter? And why do we invite suffering while we long to be happy? Starting our journey into adulthood with eagerness, we learn to modify our anticipations. There are dual forces at work influencing everything that is happening to us. Can we think of anything in this life that we may truly take for granted?

Trying to understand the contradictions of this world, the human being himself is a walking question mark — constantly assailed by the extremes within his own nature. **The mind** reveals a dual capacity: it can act as friend and counselor when it practices reason, or it can be our enemy when we are rationalizing. **Emotions** may take us momentarily from compassion to resentment, subjecting each person to the irrationalities of human relations. **Behavior** is just as easily swayed. How often do we act against our better intentions? **Character traits** are not fixed or predictable; they may worsen or improve.

We are creatures of duality, the desires of the body and the longings of the soul steadily produce conflicts within our nature. The pendulum of extremes swings back and forth, in constant motion. Coming in pairs, opposites offer a positive and a negative side:

* Knowledge is the opposite of ignorance.

* Strength is the opposite of weakness.

* Gratitude is the opposite of self-pity.

* An industrious person avoids the troubles of laziness.

* A constructive person acts purposefully and builds, instead of being self-destructive.

* You can neither be inert nor aloof if you wish to develop your potential.

The strife of the opposites accounts for the complexities of what we say and what we do. We are guided by a moral code, yet we consider our own advantages first. We live for the senses and for pleasure, yet cherish ethical beliefs. A wide gulf separates inadequate day—by—day actions from the idealized image of self. Are we to resign ourselves to these clashing contradictions? Is it impossible to achieve the harmony and peace of mind we desire? We find the answers to the perplexing riddles of our existence by exploring the dramatic swings of the pendulum.

THE PURPOSE OF DUALITY

About 370 years ago, the purpose of duality was revealed to a shoemaker who happened to enjoy the morning sun in a small German town. Jakob Boehme noticed that the sparkling rays brought the objects on his workbench picturesquely to life, while the image of the sun was reflected on the shiny surface of an old tin jug. The shoemaker was struck by the thought that the finite is inherent in the infinite... the majestic is revealed in the unassuming and modest. Jakob Boehme was so moved by these insights that he gave up his trade and eventually gained fame through his writings. He formulated the principle that everything on this earth is truly revealed by its opposite.

Everything positive gains in significance or force by its antagonist. Failure leads to success. Without pain, there would be no growth. Without the knowledge of evil the virtuous would lose its esteem. Character is built not in a time of ease and pleasure but when we are confronted with a task, a struggle, or even a tragedy.

The purpose of duality is to be liberated from ignorance. **The pendulum principle symbolizes a continuous movement towards more enlightened options:**

*   Opposites offer each person a clear choice — by recognizing the negative you may always opt for the positive. By experiencing the undesirable, you will knowledgeably pursue whatever enlightened choices appear desirable.

To be ruled by chance or to exercise control. To forever be wanting or to attain. To let happiness deteriorate or to build it in wisdom: these are your free choices.

*   *Are you, dear reader, in the habit of
     letting the opposites work for you?
     Consider the following questions:*

☐   Did a disappointment ever turn out
     to be a blessing in disguise?

☐   Were seemingly complicated problems
     ever solved by a simple solution?

☐   Can you recall lessons learned from
     a painful experience?

☐   Do you appreciate good feelings after
     having worked through a trauma?

OUTSIDE CONFLICTS

How can we sustain good feelings when we are affected by the mood swings of others? At work, our colleagues suffer from tensions; at home our companions are upset by the pull to the negative. Irritations occur when we interact with the environment. And how can we feel content in a contemporary world that thrives on strife? Civilizations, in their rise and fall, exhibit a collective consciousness which wrestles with conflicting thoughts and beliefs. Each generation rebels against its predecessor, formulating antagonistic opinions. In the modern world, upheavals are magnified by instant communication. The problem is how to cope with a climate that generates stress rather than satisfaction.... that kindles desire rather than gratitude. We wish to establish ties, friendships and a neighborly sense of belonging, but encounter uprootedness. We long for security but find ourselves in a state of transition most of the time. We seek harmony but fall prey to the pressures of an accelerated pace.

Outside forces beyond our control threaten our well-being at all times. We cannot simply shrug our shoulders and brush off the realities of pain or sorrow or injustice. We feel deeply and think about our responses to the multiple perplexing experiences that we gather. The very process of enlightenment is accompanied by growing pains. But as we wander along in contemplation, we see a graceful bridge spanning the river, a slender modern tower rising above the windblown trees or a child joyously letting its kite soar in the sky, and we wish to be part of this striving, at times triumphant humanity. We long to participate in the creative life to the best of our abilities.

POSITIVE CHOICES

To let duality work for our advantage, we must find a guide, a frame of reference. It should be as simple as possible that we may visualize our goal in a moment's recognition. It should be a constant that we may incorporate its principle into our personal value system. For this purpose I am offering you, dear reader, the dynamics of the COMFORT ZONE — your safe haven against the pull of the opposites. Whenever you feel distressed, you may regulate the pendulum of your emotions. Why not let it swing within the realm of contentment?

Getting in touch with the pendulum principle of choice gives meaning to our entire life. We are not exposed to irrational forces and senseless contradictions! Action is always followed by reaction — the contrary motion of the pendulum can be anticipated. It is orderly and predictable. We can regulate its swing and exercise control over the forces of duality. We can cope with distress by being aware of the alternative — which is feeling comfortable.

CHAPTER 1

HOW TO LIVE IN THE COMFORT ZONE

*The longest journey
starts with the first step.
(Ancient Proverb)*

The first step towards living
in my comfort zone is to like
myself because I am a growth person.

> The wise man looks inside his heart
> and finds contentment.
> (Ancient Proverb)

You and I possess only one safe haven which is immune from outside stress: THE COMFORT ZONE. It allows us to maintain a positive outlook as we move from one life cycle to the next. It offers the retreat we need to feel at ease with ourselves and at home in the world, provided that we are weaving our life into a positive pattern. Adhering to a sound set of ethics, we do not quarrel with Who We Are and What We Do. We live neither in the past nor in the future, but our energies are directed towards the present. Desires are kept under control that we do not fall victim to material pressures. Outside tensions cannot unduly invade our private island of serenity.

Does the comfort zone promise **happiness**? Or do we strive for contentment? And what is the difference? The longing for happiness is universal, but the nature of each person's desires differs. Some people succeed in generating beautiful, satisfying feelings by accepting their health and status in life gratefully. They consciously appreciate bonus pleasures: the blossoming of flowers that they planted with love and care... a stimulating evening spent with a special friend... a family holiday conducted in a spirit of harmony.

In contrast, there are those chronic seekers who depend on possessions, or on success, or on other people to make them happy. They believe that they're "unlucky" if the sunshine hours elude them. But happiness has nothing to do with luck: it is a reward - a result. It comes from being with someone in a mood of harmony, or doing something exceptionally well, or from being appreciative. It is achieved by our own efforts or predispositions. Happiness can never be a constant; it is only a transitory experience.

Contentment serves as the source of our entire well-being. We like ourselves because we are setting goals which should enhance the personality. We trust that all will be well in the future. Whenever we do experience a trauma, we transform disappointment into a learning experience and restore contentment. What, then, is the difference?

> **Happiness comes from the feeling level!** Your reason can never force you to be happy if your emotions do not go along. And your emotions can never be tuned to enjoyment if your restless mind remains dissatisfied.

> **Contentment is a frame of mind — an attitude!** It does respond to reason and is subject to your own control.

Your reasoning mind will help you to be objective should you encounter problems. It will compare advantages to disadvantages, convincing you by the sheer weight of evidence why you should be content. If ingredients are missing, reason can tell you how to better your situation. The swing of the pendulum always offers contentment. This liberating insight should fill us with confidence in the future. Should we not be able to discover whatever it might be that makes us content?

> What is the secret of happiness?
> You strive willingly and patiently
> for self-enlightenment.
> You like yourself.
> (Madame du Chene)

I-LIKE-MYSELF ATTITUDE

In essence, living in the comfort zone means that we feel neither superior nor inferior; we maintain a positive image and nourish a healthy self-esteem. Liking ourselves, we set goals, generate our own enthusiasm and derive inner security from constructive attitudes and actions. We act as our own friendly support-givers, not forgetting praise or appreciation when warranted. Self-improvers are perfectly capable of evaluating shortcomings, since they have the wisdom to be objective. They realize that everybody possesses a measure of faults as well as potentials for excellence. Feeling comfortable means accepting character weaknesses, average traits and strengths.

Character strengths bring to light our best qualities — being reliable, industrious and considerate belongs to a person's obvious assets. Character attraction can be more important to a beautiful relationship than infatuation. Once in a while you meet a person who is so magnetic that he is the center of attention. Chances are that he has consciously developed his assets and knows how to display them. Accepting our strengths in modesty can contribute to our worth as a person and act as a balance for our deficiencies.

- Am I aware of my excellent qualities?

- Do I realize that they redeem my weaknesses?

- Do they contribute to my liking myself?

- Do I compliment myself once in a while?

20

Average traits do not interfere with our feeling of comfort since we cannot excel in all facets of the personality. Our average traits are neither exceptional nor do they cause us much trouble. We are dutiful, cheerful or outgoing as a matter of habit, but do not win any championships. In keeping with the law of the opposites, we slip now and then and act selfishly. But we catch ourselves, and in monitoring our behavior we need not feel guilty. The dynamics of the opposites give us assurance: for every loss there is a compensation. Every time we learn a lesson, we gain in wisdom. We continue to improve our average traits simply by practicing self-awareness.

- Do I live comfortably with my average qualities?

- Do I appreciate that they function in harmony?

- Do they contribute to my self-confidence?

Minor weaknesses may also be accepted and need not cause the pendulum to swing beyond the comfort zone. Our objective view keeps minor flaws in perspective. Occasionally, we will be annoyed or grumpy or feel sorry for ourselves. Why not accept these little hang-ups with a sense of humor? And if we are lucky we can make them a charming aspect of the personality. I am thinking of a relative who managed to turn her thrift into a favorite family joke, poking fun at her compulsion to save used wrapping paper and pieces of string. Blessed with a sense of humor, she always laughed at her eccentricities. Since we are not striving for sainthood, let us keep realistic expectations and accept certain traits gently. Being at ease with our flaws and modest with our strengths makes others feel comfortable in our company.

☐ Am I charitable about my minor flaws?

☐ Am I careful that they cause no harm
to others?

☐ Do I trust myself to upgrade them
when necessary?

Dedicated self-improvers not only like themselves, but also trust their own judgments. Making mistakes holds no threat — whenever needed (and without feeling uptight) a few personality repairs are undertaken. Character traits and behavior are never finite, but may be upgraded at any time. Set-backs need not be exaggerated into catastrophies, but offer challenges to make the pendulum work to advantage. With such an attitude of trust, the self-improver feels secure. Behavior is predictable and energies can be freed for a productive, progressive life.

* *Do you like and trust yourself?*

1. Being vulnerable.
2. **Feeling comfortable.**

☐ Am I overly critical about myself?
☐ **Or do I view myself with compassion?**

☐ Am I striving for perfectionism?
☐ **Or am I satisfied with my best efforts?**

☐ Do I try to live up to imaginary ideals?
☐ **Or do I set attainable goals?**

☐ Do I seek praise from others?
☐ **Or do I enjoy a healthy self-confidence?**

I--LIKE--MYSELF
versus
NARCISSISM

The attitudes of liking and trusting oneself are not passed out as a gift but result from an inner growth process. We need to develop a view of the world before we realize that we function as a positive part of the whole. Excessive absorption with self prevents... rather than stimulates... the gaining of objectivity, which is why social critics have labeled the Seventies THE AGE OF NARCISSISM.

According to Greek mythology, Narcissus, son of the river god, was such a beautiful youth that he became obsessed with pride and spurned all maidens who fell in love with him. Hopelessly yearning for his affection, the mountain nymph Echo wasted away until only her voice remained... forever echoing the last words of others. As a punishment, Nemesis, the goddess of vengeance, lured Narcissus to a forest pool where he became so enchanted with his reflection that nothing could tear him away. As he reached out to his image day after day, he prayed that his own beauty would outlive him, and so he was transformed into the lovely flower Narcissus.

The modern Narcissus also has difficulties in returning affection. Living for the moment and for self-gratification, he or she is emotionally understimulated. Conditioned to seeking transitory pleasures, a gradual retreat from responsibility takes place. The gratification--seeker cannot meet the needs of others or identify with their happiness. As a result, he does not develop the inner qualities to form meaningful relationships or to make them work.

The modern Narcissus worships beauty, youth, and/or power. Fearing rejection and aging, the narcissistic conformer covers up emotional problems by placing over-emphasis on youth and beauty. Fearing failure, the power—seeker discriminates and manipulates others; he becomes so dedicated to his version of success that he falls into a life-style bent on serving self-interest with a YOU—CAN—GO—TO—HELL attitude.

The modern Narcissus has fallen in love with the psychology of the inner self. But he is unaware that he views his own personality through a distorted mirror, for self--absorption is often based on the fear of rejection and the need of approval. Taking advantage of the WHO—AM—I cult, a lot of real—me—seekers may shuttle from fad to fad and expect miracles. If they suffer from an approval-need, they undergo great efforts to make themselves attractive, believing that analyzing one's every mood and reaction might lead to self-knowledge. Other narcissists focus on their shortcomings — they view themselves as misfits who can't stand any comparison. In order that you and I, dear reader, make sure that we speak the same language, let me illustrate the differing attitudes.

THE NARCISSIST   **THE SELF—IMPROVER**

☐ Focuses on personal problems ....
.....employs the mind as
problem-solver.

☐ Sees the outer world as reactor
to the inner needs and wants...
.....has a realistic concept of
other people's priorities.

☐ Is engaged in a ME—ME—
ME preoccupation..
.....wants to liberate the mind
for other interests.

24

❑   Seeks to find self...
.....wants to lose self in a task,
in love, in service to others.

❑   Beholds an imaginary,
idealized image of self..
.... has a positive self-image as
a key to mental stability.

❑   Needs to be liked by all...
.....practices discrimination.

❑   Needs approval and praise..
.....relies on self-approval.

❑   Does not practice self-
assessment or criticism...
.....always examines own attitudes
and behavior objectively.

Self-improvers are largely unaffected by the identity-addiction and the I—DON'T—KNOW—WHO—I—AM catch-phrase, of which the author Margaret Halsey once wrote that it makes no sense unless spoken by an amnesia victim. Critics of the Decade of Narcissism view the search for normalcy as a highly elusive goal. Should not each individual come to terms with the inner needs and growth potentials? Anger, anxiety and frustration are not seen as maladjustments, just as Instant—Mental—Stability or Instant—Happiness cannot be **found**. Self-improvement can only be pursued with honesty and patience. Such philosophic foundation lies at the heart of the I—LIKE—MYSELF attitude proposed in this context.

REGULATING
THE PENDULUM

Living in the comfort zone is not a nebulous, lofty concept but an entirely attainable goal. Nobody is expected to rejoice at all times. Often we feel satisfied to get through the day with a minimum of stress, to kick off our shoes and breathe a sigh of relief, eager to close the door to the outside world. **Comfort should be the emotional yardstick to measure the degree of our well-being.**

*   *Awareness Test:*

☐   Am I in the upper range of comfort —
     perfectly happy?

☐   Am I in the medium range of comfort —
     satisfied?

☐   Am I in the lower range of comfort —
     slightly troubled perhaps, but knowing
     that my upset will soon pass?

It is perfectly normal to swing from a little sadness to pronounced joy during the course of the day. The range of comfort includes the annoyances and the elation that we experience fleetingly. We adjust and remain in control. We do not slip into a prolonged anxiety or become hyper-exhilarated. We are aware of our fluctuating feelings just as we expect clouds and rains to alternate with sunny days. At times our inner barometer indicates rain — we feel listless or lonely or misunderstood: these are perfectly normal reactions. **Measuring the degree of our comfort is the safety valve that prevents us from falling prey to the zones of extremes on either pole of the pendulum.**

To control the moment
means to control your life.
(Prince Eugene)

We do not automatically stay in our comfort zone —
we need to be self-motivators. If we experience acute distress,
it takes renewed vigor to swing the pendulum from the zone
of negativity back to contentment. **One important rule must
be followed to accomplish this goal:**

> * **It is to minimize trouble or eliminate dis-
> comfort BEFORE it turns into a major
> trauma.**

Discomfort quickly builds up and causes a negative
chain reaction. Dear reader, I wish to offer you a simple,
workable and beneficial formula. It allows you to help yourself whenever professional guidance is not warranted. **This is
how the STOP—THINK—CORRECT Healing Dynamics help
you to minimize trauma:**

STOP

Should ill feelings linger and threaten your well-being,
the first task is to stop   the build-up of a negative cycle.
SELF—AWARENESS is the key to recognizing discomfort.

THINK

After you disconnected the flow of negativity, try to
recall and evaluate the original trigger incident or the cause
of your trauma. OBJECTIVITY is the key to analyzing your
distress.

CORRECT

What can you do to restore contentment? You confront your problem... and take whatever action necessary
to correct it. SELF-MOTIVATION is the key for employing
workable alternatives until you feel in harmony.

The Pendulum Principle can be summarized as follows:
WE HAVE A FREE CHOICE. Since the pendulum swings
between two diametric opposites, we are offered a clear choice
of everything that is positive. — WE CAN EXERCISE
CONTROL. By regulating the pendulum to stay within
our comfort zone, we can avoid extremes and master our life.

> When a misfortune befalls us, ask
> yourself immediately- what power
> do I have to turn it to good use?
> (Epictetus)

A NEW OUTLOOK

The concept of duality indicates that we do not
necessarily suffer from character deficiencies of which we
should be ashamed. Why? Because it is not within our nature
to be static and one-sided. While our bodies can be defined
to the last cell, the intangible essence of the personality is
ever being influenced: learning, responding, contemplating
and growing.

Duality means that we carry some of the opposing forces within us. If it is our characteristic to be bold, we will not brashly take risks all the time but we employ caution. The bravest man may feel fear. The most patient and loving mother is confronted with situations which provoke anger. The most loving couple cannot possibly exist in total harmony.

Duality offers the clue for the incredible complexity of life. Nothing that concerns humanity can be neatly labeled and placed on a shelf. We change our opinions as our world view broadens. We understand the other person better as he explains his point of view. And we begin to understand ourselves when we confront our contradictions:

☐ Why did I experience a momentary mood swing?

☐ Why did I suddenly change my attitude?

☐ Why did I act against my better judgment?

☐ What was the cause of my personality change?

It seems that the human dilemma is not one of good or evil. **This is your true challenge: Are you a growth or a no-growth person?** No-growth people allow character traits to lie dormant. Average traits may not be a hindrance, but neither will they be upgraded to sparkle. And any minor weaknesses may turn into catastrophies.

In contrast, positive impulses predominate in the growth-people who generate their own enthusiasm and enjoy being self-motivators. Their life-long goal is to make sense out of contradictions and to stay within the positive pattern of the comfort zone.

POSITIVE CHOICES

Recognizing the laws of duality, we should not feel sorry for ourselves if desires are not promptly rewarded, but develop patience. Why not trust fate in the same manner in which we learn to trust ourselves? In the course of time we experience joy and sadness... anger and compassion... rebellion and gratitude, and desire is met with contentment. As we learn to regulate the pendulum to our advantage, we accept the negative — secure in the knowledge that it reveals and confirms the magnitude of everything positive and constructive.

CHAPTER 2

MAKING POSITIVE CHOICES

*If you can command yourself,
you can command the world.
(Chinese Proverb)*

I can make wise choices
by employing my mind as counselor.

OUR BUILT—IN COUNSELOR

We are automatically provided with an incredible and potentially infallible monitor that can help us regulate the pendulum. This free-of-charge counselor is equipped to teach us anything we truly want to accomplish:

* We can learn to be objective, realizing
when and why things go wrong.

* We can learn to analyze fairly and
logically any situation.

* We can conceive the measures needed
to eliminate distress.

* Implementing those corrective steps,
the monitor can always help us to get
back into the comfort zone.

But this counselor is only potentially infallible because it is also governed by the laws of duality! **It can direct us from a positive or negative perspective.** We are talking about the human mind and the supervisory capacities it offers the earnest self-improver IF we manage just one task: **to practice reasoning instead of rationalizing.**

THE MIND AS ENEMY
RATIONALIZING

When the intellect resorts to rationalizing it creates confusion, hides the truth and fabricates cop-outs. Rationalizing may be consciously or unconsciously applied to persuade self or others. Negative feelings feed their cues to the subjective part of the mind, which picks them up and distorts them with self-justifications, half-truths and other contrived explanations. Almost always, the purpose is to excuse, justify, defend questionable intentions... and to keep the idealized image of self intact.

Dear reader: you might not find this definition of rationalizing in your dictionary; a shift in interpretation has taken place. Invited into the expanding vocabulary of modern psychology, the term has come to mean the process of self-justification. When used in this book, RATIONALIZING always implies the distortion of truth, and BEING RATIONAL... or USING REASON serves as its positive counterpart.

No-growth people can go to extremes defending themselves... a habit that proves exhausting ·to others. Yet, we should use the term no-growth with reservation, and merely to make a point. **Let us never be tempted to look at the various types of rationalizers as hopeless cases, but merely as potential late-bloomers.** Stranger things happen than the pleasant experience of someone releasing his potential.

> *Almost all faults are more pardonable*
> *than the methods we employ to hide them.*
> *(La Rouchefoucauld)*

Chronic Rationalizers:

Negativity—dwellers like to use others as a target for their complaints. Their favorite alibi is to blame the whole world even for their smallest troubles.

Irresponsible schemers manipulate people and take advantage of their trust, ridiculing the gullibility of their victims.

Defeatists never lack for a cop-out, no matter how transparent, to excuse their lack of motivation or constructive involvement.

Ruthless strivers on the climb to the top justify their you-can-go-to-hell attitude on the competitive circumstances.

Wishful thinkers, in turn, blame these very circumstances for the failure of their fantastic plots.

There is no end to the contrived excuses used by the chronic rationalizers. But self-improvers also resort to cop-outs in order to defend weaknesses in our unguarded moments. We all are guilty of inconsistent or illogical justifications to some degree. A juxtaposition of RATIONA-LIZING versus REASONING will help us to see the difference:

RATIONALIZING   REASONING

☐   Attempts to conceal...
                            ...painstakingly seeks evidence.

☐ Justifies improper actions...
                        ...remains objective and impartial.

☐ Hides conflicts or anxieties...
                        ... employs problem-solving capacities.

☐ Aims to cover up intentions...
                        ...seeks accurate conclusions.

☐ Aims to mislead...
                        ...tries to be fair and just.

☐ Aims to cover up bias..
                        ...relies on unbiased data.

> *God has placed no limits*
> *to the exercise of the intellect*
> *He has given us.*
> *(Francis Bacon)*

THE MIND AS FRIEND
REASONING

The word REASON refers to the objective, problem-solving faculty of our mind. It represents just one aspect of our intelligence, and probably the most important one as far as our inner growth is concerned. Employing reason, we never jump to conclusions but develop a keen perception of what is fair and valid.

This is the procedure:

* To remain impartial
* To collect unbiased data
* To evaluate facts.

These are the results:

* Drawing logical conclusions
* Solving problems fairly
* Arriving at a true understanding.

The self-improvers do not give in to wishful thinking, but set their goals by weighing chances realistically. Defeat only kindles their imaginations to seek better alternatives. Cop-outs are rejected because reason reaffirms that the laws of the opposite — good fortune intermixed with a streak of bad luck — apply to everyone.

Employing reason, our life will be transformed. We learn to be critical of our feelings and attitudes. We catch ourselves whenever we are justifying faulty behavior. At last we can view ourselves objectively and admit faults because we are going to try to correct them! For the first time in our life we can be truly open-minded because we are ready to LISTEN. What is the other person trying to convey? Are we on guard against misunderstanding? Willing to consider all angles, we give others the benefit of the doubt. While shedding self-righteous attitudes, we become more loving and lovable.

Our faults irritate us to distraction
when we see them in others.
(Proverb)

WRONG: RATIONALIZING
RIGHT: REASONING

W: ☐ I am innocent, you are guilty.
R: ☐ What are the facts?

W: ☐ It's all your fault!
R: ☐ How did I contribute to the dilemma?

W: ☐ Why did you upset me?
R: ☐ Why am I responding with anger?

W: ☐ Don't tell me what to do!
R: ☐ I am willing to compromise.

THE THREE CLUE-GIVERS

"How can I find myself if I don't know who I am?"
asks the self-improver. Actually, we should know exactly who
we are, for EMOTIONS, ATTITUDES and BEHAVIOR are
constantly sending us messages or clues:

How do I feel?
What do I think?
What am I doing?

But we must carefully examine the messages, because
they are highly emotional and subjective. Trusting our emotions too much we are often unaware that they are sending
us astray. Feelings trigger actions, but do not consider consequences. Feelings reinforce attitudes, but do not control the
outcome. The three clue-givers may run riot, acting as
personality disrupters as long as they remain unsupervised —
they turn into personality builders when monitored by the
objective mind. Without its help we cannot exercise any
measure of control! As soon as reason acts as counselor, our
beliefs match our actions. Behavior is predictable and we
function in harmony. Opposites are no longer in strife...
contradictions have been reconciled, compromises reached.
We think, feel and act as integrated individuals.

☐ Do I pay attention to the messages
of my clue-givers?

☐ Do my emotions, attitudes and behavior
act as personality disrupters or builders?

☐ Am I employing my mind as
monitor-counselor?

☐ Am I in control?

Even the gods are sometimes joyous
and sometimes sad.
(Theokrit)

OUR EMOTIONS

The pendulum of extremes plays havoc with our emotions — during the course of a day they respond to myriad influences. Driving to work, a glimpse of the backlit city skyline might take our thoughts away from the tasks at hand and produce a powerful reaction. The beautiful view reminds us that the senses are continually enriched... simply by being aware. But unfortunately, we cannot keep such moments of elation running like a motor. If a careless driver cuts dangerously in front of us, good feelings are momentarily replaced with fear, and then anger.

As the day progresses, we are subject to a chain of conflicting emotions. Generally we cope very well until disturbances accumulate. If this happens we probably carry our tensions home with us and allow them to intrude in the private sphere. Perhaps we provoke a confrontation with an unsuspecting mate who is unaware of the original trigger incident and the build-up of trouble.

Emotions challenge the impulsive person to do things against all reason. How many foolish acts have been committed under the guise of love? How many crimes under the dictates of hate? Negativity—dwellers allow their fears, anxieties and depressions to run full scale. Positive extremists believe that it adds to their enjoyment to be excessively exhilarated. **But our comfort zone lies in the middle path of balance! To maintain our equilibrium, we must change course before tensions gain momentum.** We keep control by paying attention to our clue-givers, and by immediately employing the STOP—THINK—CORRECT Healing Dynamics.

STOP

☐   I am in a troubled mood and must reverse the course.

THINK

☐   I have the choice to replace boredom..........................
.....with enthusiasm.

☐   I confront my anxieties..
.....to become satisfied.

☐   I overcome inertia ....
...to feel energetic.

☐   I eliminate ill feelings..
.....and cultivate joyousness.

CORRECT

As soon as we become aware of the pendulum of choice, we replace negative feelings with their positive counterparts. We apply the same principle to our relations with the people we love — always replacing resentment with charity and compassion. Positive emotions have a chain reaction, we not only restore love, but feel good about ourselves.

REWARDS

Emotions keep us in touch with our humanity. They incite devotion to our country and worship in the warmth of our faith. They draw songs and poems from our heart. Delightedly we watch a child at play; we are filled with pleasure at a reunion with a long-lost friend. Giving in to affection and tenderness makes us feel fully alive. These are rainbow moments — the events and sights that linger on in our memory with their warm glow. So we are faced with the task of continuously upgrading our feelings that we may benefit from their healing power and safely give in to what they do best: leading us to cheer, confidence, joy and happiness.

Traveling by train through the mountains, we proceed through a long tunnel that extends for many miles. At the top of the elevation, we suddenly leave the tunnel behind and a beautiful view is revealed to our startled eyes — made even more spectacular by the contrast to the prolonged darkness. We do enjoy a similar elation when we learn to control our feelings and follow the light of reason.

> The longer we dwell on our misfortunes,
> the greater their power to harm us.
> (Voltaire)

OUR ATTITUDES

Attitudes link us to our immediate environment and to the world at large. They determine how comfortable we feel at home... what role we play in the community... and to what extent we comply with our duties as citizens. Enhancing our self-esteem, positive attitudes stimulate a more loving dialogue with the people close to us. As our world view broadens, we align ourselves with the causes that help to make this a better place for humanity.

Like emotions, attitudes also are subject to instant change — they may switch for no valid reason from generosity to prejudice or petty fault-finding. The effects of a poor frame of mind often escape detection. Since feelings are obvious and actions speak louder than words, we tend to over-look the importance of that nagging inner voice: our conscience.

Since we have a choice of attitudes we should allow others the same privilege. At all times we should give companions the benefit of the doubt. After Othello strangled Desdemona, he was presented with proof of her innocence. He listened too late to reason. Overcome by remorse, he killed himself. His feelings of jealousy kindled his deed — but his unyielding, misguided attitude and his conviction of her guilt brought about the tragedy.

As soon as we detect an objectionable attitude, we should stop to consider how we can form more charitable opinons:

STOP

Negative attitudes must be examined immediately before they trigger poor behavior. A closed mind causes a chain reaction, leading to irrational actions which in turn bring about guilt feelings.

THINK

The rationalizing mind always rallies to the defense of faulty attitudes. It allows us to place blame before we even understand the situation. We employ reason and move into the realm of objectivity.

- ☐ Am I impartial?

- ☐ Am I gathering the facts?

- ☐ Am I considering all angles?

- ☐ Am I drawing logical conclusions?

CORRECT

Attitudes are also governed by the law of the opposites:

☐   Am I biased..
.....or open-minded?

☐   Are my views cynical..
or trusting?

☐   Are my attitudes self-centered...............................
or considerate?

☐   Am I fault-finding..
or objective?

REWARDS

As our view expands we improve our attitudes by knowledge. The more we learn the further we move away from the subjective self. The more we gain in wisdom the better we relate to others. Serenity is a life-long moment-to-moment task. In this process of becoming we might abandon teachings that are not in harmony with our beliefs. Thinking and growing, we are no longer subject to conditioning outside influences. We learn to trust our judgment and we no longer need constantly to seek approval; we develop a set of values which leads us through the storm and stress of life. Our view of the world harmonizes with our beliefs. And our "judgment" of others becomes more compassionate. The reward of positive attitudes is contentment.

> *The most important human endeavor*
> *is the striving for morality in our actions.*
> *(Einstein)*

OUR BEHAVIOR

Fourteen years ago I fell in love with a puppy. She may have lost her spunkiness by now, but her companionship still contributes to my well-being. Whenever I enter the house, there she is, waiting at the door and greeting me with the utmost affection. I often marvel at the fact that in all these years nothing ever distracted her from displaying her happiness at my return. And I wonder why we humans find it difficult to show such consistent, thoroughly loving behavior. Perhaps we don't really **act** towards others, but **react** most of the time — our behavior is generally conditioned by our mood. A husband, tired from a day's work, or a wife, upset over trivialities, rarely greet one another with the warmth which would make the other simply feel wonderful.

THE CYCLE

If we can't live up to the ideal, what is in the realm of the possible? We can't merely upgrade our behavior, because it is firmly tied to how we feel and what we think. We can't merely opt for good actions if our emotions are filled with resentment, jealousy or hostility. We have no other choice but to examine the entire personality.

- Is my behavior reflecting my feelings?

- Am I acting impulsively?

- Does my behavior reflect my attitudes?

- Are my attitudes compassionate?

- Am I in a good mood because I am satisfied with my actions?

Perhaps you are wondering: whenever things go wrong, who is the culprit? Which of the three clue-givers needs the most control? Who takes the blame for upsetting the equilibrium?

STOP

Chain reactions may be triggered by the emotions, attitudes, or actions. Like a musical trio performs harmoniously, so do the clue-givers interact in unison — one influences the other. Each one carries the melody at one time or another, and as soon as you hear an out-of-tune note, you stop.

THINK

Inevitably, actions have consequences. They produce reactions from others. How do we upgrade behavior? By making positive choices because we are aware of potential outcome:

☐ My actions may be harmful...
or beneficial to others.

☐ They may be destructive...
or constructive to myself.

☐ My conduct may cause distress.....................................
or give comfort.

☐ It has negative...
or positive consequences.

CORRECT

Our actions do reflect who we are, but ONLY who we are RIGHT NOW. A person's conduct can always be improved as the total personality weaves its components into a lovelier pattern.

> Behavior is a mirror in which
> everyone displays his image.
> (J.W.v.Goethe)

Good conduct earns us esteem from others — it also reveals approval of self. Our beliefs and convictions are expressed in our deeds. We should not mystify others by speaking differently than we act. We should not change behavior like clouds before the winds or give in to elusive feelings. When our personality components are integrated, we function harmoniously — the three clue-givers make beautiful music together, while the reasoning mind serves as conductor. There is no dischord. Our emotions do not sway between exhilaration and despair. Our attitudes are supportive of self and others. And our behavior mirrors these positive feelings and attitudes.

POSITIVE CHOICES

We have set the goal to create a healthy co-existence with the duality of this world. We feel at home in our comfort zone when we govern our subjective feelings, attitudes and behavior with our objective mind. Now we should eliminate needless suffering in order to take an active part in a wholesome, creative life.

x x x x x x x x x x x x x x x x x

CHAPTER 3

TURNING WEAKNESS INTO STRENGTH

*How weak and fragile we would be
if we had no adversity.
(Anonymous)*

I can minimize trauma and transform
weakness into fortitude.

Suffering as a philosophic concept was first revealed to me in the study of classical Greek tragedy. How intimidated we were by the power of the unrelenting gods. We wondered: are the furies, those vengeful goddesses, still haunting victims to mete out justice? Since deluded man violated the cosmic order, inevitably he must suffer. To pay the consequences of his unrestrained passions, the furies punished him with tragedy and horror. But for the first time in Western history, Greek tragedy introduced an ennobling thought. Whenever man humbly accepted his fate, no matter how intolerable, he was redeemed. The harmony, upset by his selfish actions, was restored.

In contrast to this dark and troubled view of suffering, this century's various psychological movements present us with a picture of hope. We are learning that a great deal of agony is not inevitable. All too often, the unrelenting furies who perpetuate and magnify trauma originate in the mind. As a defense mechanism, we create an idealized image of self. It boosts our morale and helps us to show our best face to society. Whenever we do not live up to this image of perfec - tion, we are alarmed and suffer guilt. This means that we are torn needlessly by negative feelings while we should realize that we are presented with a choice. If suffering is self- inflicted, it can be relieved. If we are confused, we may create order. And if we fall prey to distress, we can strive for harmony.

This task is simplified by keeping two concepts in mind:

*   We should set ourselves the goal of living
       in the comfort zone — it tells us what we
       want.

*   We should replace the idealized image of
       self with that of being a self-improver.

As self-improvers we need not idealize our strengths or deny our weaknesses. We like ourselves for what we are for one important reason: we trust our own better instincts to learn from mistakes and to gain wisdom. Yes, we do leave our comfort zone whenever stress turns into distress. But we do not lose control; we can regulate the swing of the pendulum to our advantage. We do not allow ourselves to become victimized by extremes or to suffer a major trauma! On the contrary, we return to our haven of contentment as speedily as possible.

Self-improvers call upon logic to overcome discomfort; the furies are banished from the mind. We are redeemed - not by suffering an intolerable fate, but by using the powers of reason. This chapter deals with trauma that is minor and medium in degree and can be overcome readily. To this purpose, let us compare the defeatist attitudes of the no-growth-person to the constructive outlook of the self-improver.

THE NO-GROWTH-PERSON:
RATIONALIZING

> Ah yes, dear friend, it is a shame,
> No one accepts his share of blame.
> Self-righteous people always find
> A fake excuse in their own mind.
> This goes for all humanity,
> Except, of course, for You and Me.

The person caught in the wheel of rationalizing displays much ingenuity in defending self-serving attitudes. As long as blame-shifting takes place, feelings and attitudes cannot be upgraded. What seems like the easy way out is actually a web of exaggerations.

THE TAKE—ME—AS—I—AM ATTITUDE justifies lack of motivation. "You know that I'm a lovable person, why can't you overlook my being irritated?" The self-excuser refuses to communicate sensibly and pushes the cycle onward.

THE YOU—NEVER—LOVED—ME ATTITUDE is getting more dangerous; it not only shifts blame, but begins to accuse in order to keep up the self-defenses. "What's the use of trying? You never loved me and you are just waiting to find fault with me." There is a noticeable undertone of self-pity and grievences are magnified.

THE PEOPLE—ARE—NO—GOOD ATTITUDE does not allow any benefit of the doubt. Having lost all sense of judgment, the rationalizer jumps to exaggerated conclusions. Now the negative cycle affects his relationship to the whole world:

THE IT'S—A—CRUMMY—WORLD ATTITUDE signifies all-around defeat. The escapist has placed blame everywhere, except upon the source of the trouble: his own negative attitude.

THE SELF-IMPROVER:
REASONING

Self-improvers aren't saints; they also fall prey to the IT'S—A—CRUMMY—WORLD attitude when life's impositions accumulate. But they let off steam and when calming down, they try to be objective. They don't blame, accuse or condemn others outright. Realizing that they can't change the world, they try to improve their own outlook for the sake of their serenity. Tired of being absorbed in pain or worry, they work through ill feelings and return to their tasks with renewed determination.

Self-improvement is not like falling in love: it does not happen spectacularly. There is no sudden blissful moment to appreciate that we have become wise. We proceed in steps.... the growth process comes to us gradually. But the rewards are immediate: we return to our comfort zone. Having conquered the ego, we like ourselves and trust our problem-solving capacities. The secure anchor is the image of self-improvers who learn and grow.

OUTSIDE IMPOSITIONS   **MINOR TRAUMA**

Why is there no end to potential distress upsetting our equilibrium during the course of the day? We are vulnerable to the mood swings or manipulations of people with whom we come in contact at work. Whether we feel up to it or not, we have to give our best with a smiling face. While we long to relax at home, our companions' feelings would like attention. Just as we plan to use the items of convenience, they break down or need repair. And how can we end the day cheerfully, when the TV news gushes forth the catastrophies of the past twenty-four hours?

It only takes a power failure to dramatically highlight our vulnerability in this industrial world. We are actually no longer self-reliant, but dependent on mechanical forces — on the functioning of transportation, heat and light for our very existence. We hope that motors will start and machines won't sputter and die out. It's sheer luck if we are not adversely affected by the perfidity (or treachery) of the OBJECTS — an interesting concept exploited in German literature and the silent films of the Golden Age. According to this theory, objects have dynamic forces, or an insiduous life of their own, causing us to lose our composure... diabolically dominating or haunting us, and wreaking havoc with our serenity in countless mysterious ways. We leave our comfort zone when accumulated stress turns into distress! As a result of the overload, the pendulum swings into the realm of negativity.

Since we can't afford to dissipate our energies wastefully, we have to develop a protective shield.

Can we increase our capacity to endure stress? The breaking point differs from person to person. The quitter exhibits little tolerance and becomes frustrated; the perseverer views difficulties as a challenge.

Is the trigger incident a triviality? Most of the time, the minor trauma we experience is not caused by us — we are not responsible for any harm to anybody. All we are doing is REACTING to an unpleasant incident. But how arc wc reacting? Are we brooding over it? Are we exaggerating the significance? Are we allowing a negative cycle to brew?

Can we promptly dismiss the trauma from our mind? If we can't rise above it immediately, we should verbalize the incident to an understanding companion who gives us support and helps us to regain perspective. We should then forget it.

To succeed with these goals, the self-improver refers to the reasoning mind as counselor and employs the STOP—THINK—CORRECT Healing Dynamics:

STOP

We stop brooding immediately, disconnect the flow of negativity and call on the objective mind to replace rationalizing with reasoning:

THINK

The degree of discomfort serves as a yardstick: the less severe the anguish, the easier it is to restore harmony.

- ☐ Does my trouble prevent me from concentrating on my duties?

- ☐ Is it harming my relationships?

- ☐ Is it threatening my zest of life?

The significance of the trigger incident must be analyzed -- is it of any consequence to the future?

- ☐ Am I brooding over a minor grievance?

- ☐ Am I over-reacting?

- ☐ Will this be of consequence in ten years, in ten days or even tomorrow?

CORRECT

Is the trigger incident a triviality?

- ☐ Can I forget it right now?

It is time to pay yourself a compliment for the sucessful return to the comfort zone.

- ☐ Do I like myself because I have conquered a negative cycle?

- ☐ Do I trust myself to avoid similar incidents in the future?

But what about the next incident that will happen tomorrow? Perhaps we simply have to be prepared. Minor upsets are as certain as the clouds hiding the sun. Our experience and wisdom prepare us to expect the other people's pendulums to swing to the negative side, and we should try to prevent their personality disrupters from invading our comfort zone.

MEDIUM TRAUMA
SELF-GENERATED

Whenever we fail to regulate the pendulum of our character traits, our problems begin to make waves. Perhaps we feel dissatisfied for any number of reasons. Perhaps the ego acts as a villain, disrupting pleasant relationships. Or faulty attitudes are throwing stumbling blocks to our well-being. Are we ruled by resentment or greed? Then we cease to behave predictably because ill feelings distort our actions.

Whenever this happens, others are usually involved, and we are apt to hurt their good will. Feeling guilty, our own discomfort increases. We are suffering a MEDIUM TRAUMA that is more difficult to correct — it warrants honest soul-searching and the admission of fault! In this process of trial and error learning we may, like the dedicated scientist in his laboratory, discover hundreds of ways that do NOT work. At last we find a behavior solution which is just right for us. It takes time to test and know how we respond to various situations, and the errors that happen should not be regarded as failures, but as stepping stones to success. This attitude helps in our soul-searching task.

People hate to admit having a weakness — they believe it to be a character deficiency. The truth is often far less dramatic. When we leave our comfort zone, our emotions and attitudes experience an upset. The positive qualities swing to the negative side!

54

Let us say you are liked for your good qualities: being stable and modest, thoughtful and considerate. Friends know they can count on your compassion. Coping with the day-to-day routines, you display the flexibility of a sensible person. Appreciating your well-being, you are content. This means that you are blessed with the following attributes:

Compassion
Patience
Contentment
Gratitude
Modesty
Thoughtfulness
Flexibility

Now let these beautiful qualities become agitated because ill feelings are not controlled, and they cannot do anything else but turn into their opposites:

STRENGTH		WEAKNESS
Compassion	⟺	Anger
Patience	⟺	Intolerance
Contentment	⟺	Greediness
Gratitude	⟺	Self-pity
Modesty	⟺	Vanity
Thoughtfulness	⟺	Selfishness
Flexibility	⟺	Rigidity

The pendulum swings to the negative side and the opposite of each virtue takes over:

☐   We are no longer filled with compassion.....................
                because we have failed to control anger.

☐   Exhausting our patience, ...
                we get intolerant.

☐   Whenever we fail to practice contentment, ...
                we are prone to becoming greedy.

☐   Whenever we do not feel appreciated, ...
                gratitude readily swings to self-pity.

THE MIND AS ENEMY

Something is happening inside which we don't like, and in self-defense we blame the companions whom we hold responsible for this change in feeling. We are rationalizing!

☐   Do I blame others, when I should be
      taking a good look at myself?

☐   Do I find it difficult to admit my faults?

☐   Do I pretend others won't notice my
      weaknesses if I rationalize them away?

☐   Do I find it difficult to say:
      'I am sorry!'?

Instead of solving problems, we are resorting to the TAKE-ME-AS-I-AM attitude of the rationalizer. Behaving immaturely, we fail to let reason act as a monitor. When this happens, let us get in touch with our two goals: we wish to return to our comfort zone..... and we can do it, because we are self-improvers!

STOP

☐   I have given in to a faulty behavior pattern.
Can I stop the negative build-up?

THINK

☐   Which poor habit or shortcoming caused my distress?

CORRECT

☐   Did I restore good will be offering an apology?

PREVENT

☐   Do I trust myself to prevent similar incidents
in the future?

We have reversed the swing of the pendulum and our virtues have re-asserted themselves! The demeaning anger is spent before it caused major damage... and is replaced with compassion and tolerance. Greediness or self-pity have given way to contentment and gratitude.

POSITIVE CHOICES

We can minimize trauma by being aware. Understanding the language of our feelings, we stop generating a negative cycle at the onset. In touch with our image as self-improvers, we correct present — and prevent future — problems. But we should not set our goals in a frantic, extreme effort to turn into a saint. Why not take the example of a veteran gardener? He pulls weeds to plant his favorite flowers. Let's compliment ourselves and appreciate the results, as we succeed in beautifying the inner landscape.

My great concern is not whether you have failed,
but whether you are content with your failure.
(Abraham Lincoln)

CHARACTER STRENGTH

Everytime we succeed in turning a weakness into a strength, our personality becomes enriched. At the same time, we possess levels of strength of which we might be unaware because they have not yet been tested.

☐   Can I rely on my strength?

☐   Can others rely on me?

☐   Am I trying to increase my strength?

Some people are blessed with a fortitude and determination that go beyond the imaginable. We need only think of Helen Keller — blind, deaf, mute. She refused to be intimidated and led a life of service, becoming an inspiration. Think of Beethoven who composed and conducted his Ninth Symphony in total deafness. We read contemporary stories of average people who conquer crippling hardships to lead full lives. We respond with awe to the human being's capacity of not being defeated, in order to accomplish the miraculous.

The same phenomenon is at work collectively. Historians have observed that hardships (such as floods, earthquakes or war) promote unity, strength and fortitude. There is a common enemy to be conquered: nations rally, rise above the ordinary, and people become heroic. During the last war in Europe, citizens — as a matter of course — risked their lives to save others during the nightly bombings.

This seems to indicate that human beings, individually or collectively, possess a vast reservoir of strength which is often allowed to lie dormant. Only if our survival instincts are threatened or a cataclysmic trauma befalls us do we operate at full potential. Crisis or loss often brings out the best in us and at such times of drawing together, we are capable of an unselfish love and support. Whenever we do release the energies held in reserve, we help others and accomplish more than we imagined.

But not everyone finds the key to unlock inner strength. Much as in the drama of ancient times, human passions still lead to tragedy. Whenever excesses cannot be modified, a major trauma inevitably occurs. It brings suffering and despair not only to the victim, but to the loving members of the family.

CHAPTER 4

NOTHING TO EXCESS

We always weaken
whenever we exaggerate.
(J.F.deLaharpe)

I trust myself to avoid extremes
and to stay within the boundaries
of my comfort zone.

*"Our love of the things of the mind
does not make us soft."*

During its time of glory, ancient Greece discovered the importance of the mind as we understand it today, and the legacy we inherited is to KNOW THYSELF. Along with the striving for self-knowledge, Greeks worshipped **moderation.** They inscribed the words **NOTHING TO EXCESS** onto the Temple of Delphi... to remind themselves not to give in to temptation. Practicing excess means to leave the comfort zone and to succumb either to the negative or positive extreme. Whenever people become victims of chronic excess, a major trauma results.

MAJOR TRAUMA

Every life holds an infinite promise. There is the lovely baby growing into an adult who is precious to his family. His parents watch over him with pride and joy. They try to instill values, to make him a confident human being. Do they always provide the best possible guidance? It is easy to love and reward, but hard to discipline effectively. Giving their best, they hope that their child is equipped to handle the vicissitudes of life.

And then, some parents fall prey to a heartbreaking trauma. Withdrawing from reality and not accepting the challenges of confronting obstacles, their son or daughter becomes a victim of addiction and is set on the tragic path of self-destruction. How did it happen?

For the addictive or overly sensitive persons things may go wrong if they fail to receive the positive reinforcement they need early in childhood. Things go wrong if a sense of futility cannot be transformed into its postive counterpart. Or perhaps the resilience is lacking to overcome minor problems. The self-assured person gets into his IT'S—A—CRUMMY—WORLD attitude for a while and then dismisses trivialities. The alcoholic uses the same set of circumstances to remove himself further from coping. **When minor traumas go unattended, and when coupled with self-destructive tendencies, they catapult into major trauma and threaten survival.**

It is a matter of becoming. Just as we become wiser and more giving, so does the escapist become more depressed and more isolated in a gradual decline. Poor attitudes, if allowed to magnify, threaten relationships and lead to isolation. They keep the malcontent in a state of hostility. To relieve his tense mind, he turns to substitutions.

People often think: "What is so terribly wrong with indulging my weaknesses? Aren't they harmless little eccentricities?" Maybe so, but as soon as the escapist — refusing to confront and correct - starts to substitute, he invites trouble. One person boozes when upset, the other finds gratification by stuffing down food, the next heads to the single's bar for a night of indiscriminate sex with a stranger. How few of us are realizing that these persons simply are attempting to still the nagging voice of their own psychic pain: they need to find out that they are lovable. Can they turn the pendulum of their lives around? Can they free themselves from the mental barriers which prevent them from becoming self-improvers? They would need to accept the message that they are worthy of love... and that the way they conduct their lives is important.

THE NEGATIVE EXTREME -
THE ZONE OF DISTRESS

When people have left the comfort zone, they may not admit their problems, but they no longer like themselves.... which is the basic cause of their depression. Not controlling their negative—extremist tendencies, they become unable to judge their behavior and the effect it has on others. Chronic negativity—dwellers may live predominantly on the negative side of the pendulum for decades, disrupting everyone's chances for happiness. The failure to exert a measure of self-discipline demands what seems to be an unduly high price.

What types of negativity—dwellers do we have in mind?

Negativity—Dwellers

The self-pitier fancies that everyone is deeply interested in his tale of woe.

The chronic worrier is too busy worrying to notice any pleasant event.

The chronic self-doubter feels that he is not worthy of good fortune.

The martyr derives something akin to pride in enduring miseries.

The masochist goes one step further and invites miseries with a neurotic willingness.

The negative extremist overindulges first and has guilt complexes later.

THE MIND AS ENEMY
RATIONALIZING

Chronic negativity—dwellers need as much positive reinforcement as the extremists—prone—to—addiction. Since the feelings of self-esteem can only be self-generated, extremists must realize the need to confront and correct faulty attitudes (which would be speeded along by receiving professional help). Where should they start? Which personality traits need upgrading? Most likely, the no-growth-persons are set on a pattern of rationalizing. Focusing on their own small world, they perpetuate a WHY—DID—THIS—HAPPEN—TO—ME attitude which stifles inner growth. Protecting their fragile egos, they do not admit mistakes, even when confronted with evidence.   Negativity—dwellers also tend to lack patience. Unable to bear annoyances or delays, they dissipate energies at the start of the race and drop out when others gain momentum.

HOW TO LIVE WITH
NEGATIVITY DWELLERS

Unfortunately, the negativity—dweller is often a dependent type... a clinger. Beset by fears and feelings of inadequacy, he "cannot make it in the world out there" and seeks security from others. He feels lonely in his own company and stays attached to those who are strong and positive. You, the self-improver, will be adversely affected by living with a no-growth-person. Your patience and good intentions will be sorely tested. You must minimize the interference with your well-being. Think of the story of the village where the unfortunate were helped not by being provided with fish... but by being taught how to gain their livelihood by fishing. For your own serenity, realize what you should and should not do.

* Do carry the message of hope, but do not carry
  the person.

* Do not reinforce negativity, and do not
  patronize immaturity.

* Do not bail out the chronic negativity—dweller.

* Do not pay for the consequences of his
  behavior.

He has a right to his negative attitude, but he also has the right to learn from his mistakes. You may hope that eventually the no-growth-person may opt for the building of character by the sheer force of your good example. This is not an idle hope. I remember how impressed I was the first time I heard the concept of "planting seed thoughts". Some people need many seed thoughts for a few to take hold. Others experience a long interval before blossoming occurs. And sometimes, a spectacular flowering takes place after it is no longer expected. Time works in your favor.

Objectivity and patience may be obtained when enough seed thoughts ... plus painful experiences bring home the message. Such transformations happen when a person changes his life-style, switching from greed to service. An alcoholic may accept the A.A.'s message of hope and turn crusader. The lure of constructive living proves powerful; the more the chronic negativity—dweller seeks escape, the deeper is his longing to embrace the healing forces of contentment. To keep planting seed thoughts in a loving or charitable attitude is the best gift the self-improver can offer.

FROM ONE EXTREME
TO THE OTHER

We must realize that the zones of discomfort also encompass stages or degrees. A person's outlook may drive him to self-indulgences for decades, while he may still keep body and soul functioning. On the other hand, a compulsive extremist may practice excess to excess and burn himself out.

Always, the danger is one of progression:

*   from leaving the comfort zone —

*   to becoming a negative or positive extremist entrapped in a destructive pattern —

*   to a final breakdown.

In the early part of this century, Paris was the birthplace of modern art and the young Italian Amedeo Modigliani belonged to its pioneers. His intensely personal style could immediately be recognized. His paintings – superbly crafted portraits with simplified features and a swan-like neck — are now among the cherished possessions of the world's great museums. During his short, poverty-stricken life, the gifted artist was reduced to making his rounds of the Paris bistros, sketching a likeness for anyone who, out of pity, would buy him a drink. Most people would discard his work, never imagining that upon Modigliani's death it would be worth fabulous sums. By nature, the artist was a sufferer. Unable to shake off melancholy, he swung to the opposite extreme, seeking euphoria in mad bouts with drugs and alcohol. He burned himself out and died at the age of thirty-five.

The two extreme poles share a reverse relationship: one represents the flip side of the other. Equally removed from mid-center, they no longer fall into the norm. This explains why all too often escape is sought through substitutes. The negative extremist may become addicted in order to relieve the agonies of his mind. The positive extremist is driven to dramatic pendulum swings because euphoria proves fleeting and is inevitably followed by depression. The vicious cycle may start innocently enough with attitudes that do not embrace balance as the ultimate ideal.

THE POSITIVE EXTREME: THE ZONE OF EXCESS EXHILARATION

When we are young, we believe that emotions reign supreme. "Feelings are everything!" exclaimed the young Goethe, Germany's greatest poet, and a literary movement developed which called itself Storm and Stress (with the word 'stress' implying desire, or passion). The movement influenced the ideals and manners of youth throughout Europe. The intensity of its sentimental excess can be compared to America's youthful ideologies of the Sixties, when similar romantic notions became the vogue. If feeling deeply is desirable... then should not exuberance be even better? Does not a state of exhilaration make us feel more fully alive? In his later years of Olympian wisdom, Goethe turned away from the exhilaration excesses of his youth. He sought balance and moderation in his way of life and paid homage to harmony in his work.

While the negative extremist is drawn to gloom, the positive extremist yearns for euphoria, the magic land where all difficulties dissolve in a nebulous glow of exhilaration. It is not uncommon that some people's pendulum swings from one extreme to its diametric opposite.

A similar transformation happens to us when we mature
— we no longer sway along wherever the mood takes us. As we
grow older and wiser, we learn by experience that the cautious
outlook is more productive. We come to cherish the balance
which allows us to function at our maximum potential. We
welcome the positive state — but not beyond the range of our
comfort zone.

    *   *Does your pendulum swing to emotional excess?*

    *   Am I given to extreme mood swings?

    ☐   Do I feel listless unless in a state of excessive
emotions?

    ☐   Do I resort to artificial stimuli to feel "high"?

    ☐   Do I believe there should be no limits to
exuberance?

When living with a positive extremist, the self-improver
must recognize the symptoms which the sufferer refuses to admit. Understanding the underlying mentality can help —
exhilaration extremists are untrained to use their positive
energies constructively and remain dedicated to the violence
of excess. In love with excitement, they are not satisfied
with feeling good, but must be aroused from peak to peak.

Exhilaration Extremists

Thrill-seekers become emotionally dependent on
escalation and need to generate a torrid atmosphere.

Escapists derive no satisfaction from the simple, everyday joys of a "humdrum" life. They deny the importance of their potential contribution to society.

Wishful thinkers create an emotional high by chasing one unworkable scheme after the other. They lack the patience to work diligently towards an orderly plan.

Chronic losers drift from opportunity to opportunity. The mind's chief preoccupation centers around where and how to obtain the next bottle or fix.

Zealots need to preach euphoria if they are born leaders. If they are followers, they display fanatical devotion to their leader who rescued them from unworthiness and instilled them with a sense of identity or mission or mystical union.

SOCIETY

We are living in a strange society. After it has done its best to tempt and weaken, it goes all out to make amends. Social drinking and martini luncheons have become a national pastime. The working population is subjected to the pressures resulting from the priority motivation of "profit as the bottom line". Does an overly high percentage of Americans seek addiction as a refuge? Do vulnerable people retreat from an environment that overtaxes inner strength? Competition in itself is addictive and compulsive. The individual must become aware of its impact on his life.

In this context, we should realize that the very concept of the American Dream has been subject to a positive and negative interpretation. Its original meaning centered around dedication to freedom... to providing a sanctuary for the poor and unfortunate. In the course of time, the Dream became synonymous with achieving happiness through material acquisition. Prosperity for its own sake was no longer sufficient; it had to produce an ever-accelerating upward curve. We need to reconcile the two viewpoints of individual freedom versus an enslaving materialism. The goal of prosperity should not produce a life-style of intense competition, tension and anxiety. Only when the proper balance occurs will the American Dream truly be fulfilled. In the meantime, we, the involved individuals, must create a personal haven where we can nourish our humanity. We must find ways to extricate our professional lives from excessive pressure.

LIFELINES

On the other side (and here we observe the paradox of human nature), the United States is probably the most generous nation on earth. The desire to conquer calamities, to stretch out a helping hand, has created a nationwide network of charitable groups.

Whenever an addiction-trauma occurs professional help should be sought immediately. We are fortunate that assistance is offered not only to sick persons, but also to the members of the family who are being taught how to cope. Occasionally you hear a critic of the self-help-movement poking fun at the emphasis on sharing. Actually, this kind of sharing in times of utter distress is what progress is all about. For every addiction or illness there has been a volunteer group created to provide guidance. Obtain a directory of your community service organizations, and you will meet the knowledgeable people who will provide the needed support.

We are in bondage to the law
in order that we may be free.
(Cicero)

THE LAW OF PURPOSE
AND RECONCILIATION

Having examined the various traits that characterize the zones of extremes, the reader may ask:"How does this effect me? I experience similar mood swings, ranging from a fleeting depression to exuberance during the course of a day. Does this mean that I am an extremist?" The concept of duality provides a reassuring answer. It seems that life tosses the waves of contrast onto the shores of our being that we may experience the whole of it. Is there not a redeeming purpose in knowing weakness and frailty? We develop a more compassionate attitude to our fellow-sufferer, which is expressed in the saying: "There, but for the grace of God, go I." Many miracles are worked due to the existence of duality and it accomplishes many purposes:

* TO DISCOVER A BETTER FORMULA:
Extremes are compressed into new discoveries, as validated by science and philosophy. Thesis produces counterthesis which leads to synthesis --- a new compound or wholeness.

* TO STIMULATE PRODUCTIVITY:
Extremes are utilized for a benefit. As creativity is stimulated, workable solutions emerge and productivity increases.

* TO ACHIEVE UNITY:
Diversity leads to unification. As a melting place of all races and creeds the United States is weaving its diversity into a homogenous whole.

* TO RECONCILE DIFFERENCES:
Frugality and extravagance can be reconciled by a happy balance. Fanaticism in either direction should lead to neutrality and objectivity.

* TO ACHIEVE HARMONY:
We need to minimize absurdities for the sake of good sense, that we may live in harmony.

It is natural, therefore, to expect extremes in our personal lives. The death of a parent leaves a void that cannot be filled and produces a time of excessive sorrow. It may also fill us with a new maturity and with insights that we may utilize in our relationships with others. There are highlight times in our lives — as in a young marriage, or following the birth of a baby, or during a long expected voyage — when we consciously cherish an emotional intensity. But in the course of our daily routine, the purpose and task is to make duality work to our advantage, and to stay in control of fluctuating emotions — mindful of their dangerous pull.

POSITIVE CHOICES

The pendulum of extremes showers upon us a life of incredible richess and diversity. As the poet said, we may experience heaven and hell right here on this earth. But duality always provides us with a choice. Whenever extremes or differences are reconciled for the sake of a higher purpose — whenever the choice is made for the positive — individuals and nations gain immeasurably.

CHAPTER 5

THE WISDOM OF BALANCE

*We should begin by practicing moderation
that we may feel comfortable.
(J.W.v. Goethe)*

I can turn the pendulum of opposites
to my advantage by choosing excellence.

While positive or negative extremists invite major trauma, self-improvers strive for balance. They stay in their comfort zone by letting the pendulum swing from absurdity to common sense, from right to wrong, from failure to success. But sometimes it requires more insight to regulate extremes. Sometimes both opposites are undesirable and we have to find the midpoint of balance or excellence. For example, the opposite of asceticism or self-denial is indulgence. Neither extreme proves desirable — the point of excellence is found in moderation. We are reminded of an historical figure who lived a life of incredible extremes, before he was able to enlighten mankind about the wisdom of the Middle Way.

> From Good must come Good
> and from Evil must come Evil.
> (The Buddha's First True
> Law of Life)

Along the slopes of the Himalayas in the far northeast of India, the Gautama Buddha preached the doctrines which have survived to this day as Buddhism. He was said to be the last and the greatest in a succession of historical Buddhas (Enlightened Ones).

As a young prince, Gautama Siddharta received the finest education and was brought up with all the luxuries and enticements, the wealth and power that his father, the king, could command. But one day the prince became distressed by a life of festivities and pleasures. He left the lavish palaces, gave up his wealth and exchanged his jewels and beautiful robes for a beggar's garment and bowl. For seven years he wandered along dusty mountain roads, visiting the sages who lived in caves to better pursue wisdom. The beggar-monk tried to find answers to the questions: Why are we here? Where do we come from? Where are we going?

74

Fasting and praying, exposed to poverty and suffering, he sought enlightenment until he was too weak and sick to continue. One day, lying under a Banyon tree, he tried to understand why both unlimited pleasure and extreme self-denial had failed to give him wisdom. He had been a prince which taught him that the sole pursuit of pleasure was not worthy of a noble soul. Renouncing wealth by his own free will, he had become a beggar-monk. Would retreat from the world and absolute poverty purify his soul? But rather than enlightening him, self-denial only made him too weak to even think. Now he realized that he must find enlightenment within himself by resuming an active, sharing life. He decided to teach and became the Buddha.

One of the ideals not apparent in the traditions he knew was the Doctrine of the Middle Way: the light to which mankind should be led. The Buddha preached avoidance of the extremes of selfish pleasure and unworthy self-torture. 2500 years ago, the rejection of diametric opposites was incorporated into the world's first truly universal religion.

We choose honor, pleasure, intellect
because we believe that through them
we shall be made happy.
(Aristotle)

THE GOLDEN MEAN

A hundred years after the death of the Buddha, one of Western Civilization's most extraordinary thinkers, Aristotle, was born near Athens. He conceived the rules of reasoning by gathering evidence, drawing up distinctions and arriving at conclusions. His philosophic universe is so logical and balanced that it seems to contain the best possible common-sense approach.

Not many philosophers regard happiness as a goal, but Aristotle taught that all actions should provoke a good feeling. What is happiness? According to Aristotle, not a life of pleasure but an unfolding of one's essential nature striving to develop all facets of the personality. We become proficient by practicing good habits. Since thought is the most remarkable capacity, excellence in reasoning should lead to happiness.

The Greek philosopher gave us a guide to satisfactory conduct in his concept of the Golden Mean. It is a dynamic process of BECOMING: each thing represents a potentiality which moves through a development to an actual truth. The purpose is to reconcile contradictions and to achieve balance by chosing the Middle Path.

VIRTUES IN THE LIGHT OF DUALITY

It may seem strange that our positive qualities are tested by the stress of the opposites. Life is a stern task-master and teaches that idealism must be tempered with a healthy injection of realism. We like to be optimistic, but experience warns us that at times pessimism can be warranted. To be trusting is a beautiful quality, but we may invite disappointment if we do not practice some skepticism. **This means that virtues need a balancing element, a critical counterpart.**

Virtues need control. The pendulum principle reveals a startling phenomenon: when a virtue leaves the comfort zone and shoots off into the zones of excess, it becomes exaggerated. It is no longer a virtue but turns into a vice. We observe the REVERSE RELATIONSHIP of extremes:

76

Reverse Relationship of Extremes:

* The negativity-dweller's vices need upgrading
that they may turn into virtues.

* The positive extremist's virtues need discipline
to prevent them from becoming vices.

BALANCE IS ALWAYS REACHED AT THE MIDPOINT:

COMFORT ZONE

NEGATIVE EXTREME ⟺ ⟺ POSITIVE EXTREME

VICE ⟺ ⟺ EXAGGERATED VIRTUE

⥯

If you possess the following virtues, consider
what happens when they are exaggerated-

Modesty	⟺	Humiliation
Caution	⟺	Immobility
Determination	⟺	Obstinacy
Generosity	⟺	Extravagance
Loyalty	⟺	Submission
Self-Control	⟺	Rigidity

Virtues turned into Vices

VIRTUES carried to excess may cause more harm than vices for they are much harder to detect. People seem generally aware of their strengths but do not realize when an exaggerated virtue turns into a weakness. How can you know if you are displaying willpower or if you are just being obstinate? How can you tell if you are being cautious or indecisive?

A VICE, therefore, is not corrected by falling into its opposite extreme. Instead we aim for the middle position which represents its true virtue. Aristotle's Golden Mean reveals that the desirable alternative to either extreme is excellence, the virtue which stops short of becoming exaggerated.

NEGATIVE EXTREME:	Indecisiveness
VIRTUE:	Determination
POSITIVE EXTREME:	Obstinacy

Let us suppose arrogance has been called to a person's attention and he is anxious to correct it. Acutely self-conscious, he might easily overcorrect. He might act overly humble or subject himself to humiliation. The true virtue would be modesty, which stops short of being humble. No wonder that we are faced with difficulties to be virtuous, **for a good quality has not one, but two opposites — a negative extreme (a vice) and a positive extreme (an exaggerated virtue).**

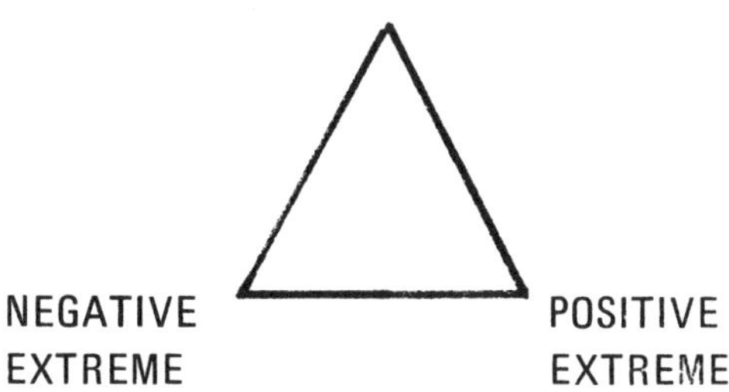

This explains the startling contradictions of people. For example, millionaires are known to swing from extravagance to stinginess. Heinrich Schliemann made three fortunes so he could spend it lavishly on the pursuit of his childhood dream: the discovery and excavation of the fabled ancient city of Troy. He hired as many as 150 laborers a day to dig up archeological sites — yet he advised his wife (whom he loved dearly) to dine at a different restaurant in order to save thirty cents. And a famous millionaire of our time, who presided over thousands of employees, spent enormous sums on art projects for public use. Yet one of his office managers told me they had to account to him directly for the pencils each department used.

NEGATIVE EXTREME:	Avarice
VIRTUE:	Generosity
POSITIVE EXTREME:	Extravagance

I know a health extremist whose sole aim in life is keeping fit. He is regularly driven to indulge in junk-food orgies, which causes him severe anguish afterwards.

NEGATIVE EXTREME:	Self-indulgence
VIRTUE:	Self-control
POSITIVE EXTREME:	Self-denial

STOP

Whenever we detect extremist behavior, we stop to regulate the swing of the pendulum.

THINK

☐   Am I aware of my virtues?

☐   Do I stop at the point of excellence?

☐   Do I tend to carry a virtue to its positive extreme?

☐   Can I distinguish a positive from a negative extreme?

CORRECT

☐   I will avoid excess and find the midpoint of balance.

We should now consider a problem of particular relevance to our civilization: the extremes of over- and under-achieving. The Golden Mean is symbolized in the attitudes of the achiever.

UNDER-ACHIEVERS

We do not have any group (be it sex, age or race) in mind when we think of the under-achievers, but picture timid persons unaware of their potential. The super-charged climate of the working world bewilders and overwhelms. The process of finding a job can be ego-shattering. The certain amount of healthy self-advertising needed to free-lance, or to impress an employer, or to advance is something that cannot be adequately handled.

The under-achievers' professional handicaps are most likely associated with their personal problems. They face the task of gradually building potentials: perhaps of becoming assertive, or self-motivated, or of gaining expertise. They must learn to create a life-style that is best suited to their inclinations. We all share reponsibility in creating an overly competitive climate and should seek solutions to this problem in a collective effort.

OVER-ACHIEVERS

Far more common in our profit-oriented society is the malaise of being an over-achiever. Ambitions start out as a plus; they motivate us to do something with our life. But they easily zoom out of control; competitive strivers become obsessed with their varying notions of success. Over-achievers throw their whole energies into their work and along the way, something unappetizing happens to their values. Defending their place on the top, they rationalize that intimidating others is the modus operandi of today's capitalism. The mind set on power, they get entrenched into a state of psychological warfare with anyone considered a threat. Always conscious of manipulating people, they know when to be tough and abusive, when to placate others and when to flash a trustworthy smile. They are so out of touch with the real world that they fantasize such lowly objects as a lock on a cabinet to be a power symbol (along with an elaborate set of rituals). Over-achievers have the consolation of being a success at the office, but they seem to be one-dimensional in their private sphere. Later in life — should it become their turn to be pushed aside—despair sets in. Realizing that their best years have slipped by, they discover the void in the areas of love, growth, family, intimacy, friendship and other needs.

ACHIEVERS

We do not measure achievers by their money or status. Equating their image with that of the average American, we are thinking of people who lead a good, fulfilling existence in whatever circumstances they are placed. They like to be productive, enjoy their work and do their duties to the best of their abilities (which provides them with a true sense of satisfaction). They select working situations which offer the dignity of a private life. Achievers realize the necessity of balance and enjoy a wide variety of pleasurable interests, trying to cultivate all-roundedness in their leisure time. They consciously minimize worry by being discriminating; they develop immunity to the lure of advertising and avoid being entrapped in a credit-card life-style.

The consciousness revolution which erupted in the Sixties and attacked the standard work ethic jostled traditions. Following the lead of their women, American men also took a good look at themselves and detected an obligatory functioning as supercharged providers. ("I discoverd that I was reduced to a yes-saying workaholic. Who needs it?") Realizing that there is a better choice than collapsing after an overtime-filled work-week, men have become concerned with improving the quality of their lives. As a paradoxial development, the power-seeking corporate woman emerged, exhilarated by the new air of freedom and eager to step into the shoes of the corporation executive who had become the target of ridicule during the Sixties. So we have the irony that a group of women are seeking the American symbols of success (status, money, power) while men are comtemplating more meaningful priorities. Though the images keep changing, society sets up ideals to be emulated. The achiever tries to conform to society's values, but knows when to be discriminating. Call it success or balance or the Golden Mean: the wholesome man and woman build a positive pattern in all dimensions of life, not shortchanging the essentials for the sake of materialism. We are currently experiencing an inner freedom and maturity entirely new in the nation's development — it includes the courage to interpret success in an unorthodox, personal, meaningful way.

STRIVING FOR BALANCE

In our eagerness to achieve harmony, let us remember that Aristotle did not counsel perfection. Once we make up our mind to pursue excellence, we can do no less. Anything that the unique personality incorporates into its value system becomes an accepted ideal and we try to live up to it. Can we strive for a life-style of excellence? Ideally, we should creatively balance work and play, solitude and fellowship, the need to love and the need to grow as a human being. Our professional and private activities offer an opportunity for perpetual goal-setting.

Stimulating the mind should be as much a routine as finding time for recreation and leisure. We need to refresh our spirits by getting away from crowds and noises and mediocre city streets, to wander along nature's path, sit at the edge of a murmuring stream, simply watching the formation of clouds and the interplay of the sun on shimmering leaves. In previous centuries, families remained in touch not only with nature's cycles, but also with creature life. And how can we appreciate balance without fun and humor? Being able to swing the pendulum from sullenness to laughter and good cheer is like moving from the shadow into the sun. Allow yourself to be lighthearted, to laugh in abandon like a child and to cultivate joyousness for these are the happiest expressions of a balanced personality.

*Tell me how you keep busy
and I will tell you who you are.
(Goethe)*

* **Checklist: Considering balance at
the end of one day —**

☐   Did I give and receive love?

☐   Were my relationships harmonious?

☐   Did I satisfy my friendship/fellowship needs?

☐   Did I enjoy my work?

☐   Did I take good care of my body?

☐   Did I stimulate my mind?

☐   Did I laugh? Was I joyous?

☐   If my present life-style is inadequate,
how can I achieve a better balance?

The Buddha's Middle Way and Aristotle's Golden Mean have retained their powerful force. They proved to be universal truths, because they are uncomplicated and self-evident:

*	To develop the personality's potential by striving for excellence;

*	To avoid unhealthy extremes by choosing the ultimate virtue;

*	To find happiness by leading a harmonious life.

We not only recognize such universal truths, but accept them as a guiding light for our own personal growth.

ᘒ ᘒ ᘒ ᘒ ᘒ ᘒ ᘒ ᘒ ᘒ ᘒ ᘒ ᘒ

CHAPTER 6

CYCLES AND TRANSITIONS

*Life is the childhood
of our immortality.
(Goethe)*

I have the choice to view
my life as a cycle of
meaningful progressions.

Rousseau made this cynical remark about civilized man:

At ten he is led by cakes,
at twenty by a mistress,
at thirty by ambitions,
at forty by avarice.
When does he make wisdom
his sole pursuit?

Nobody has been able to figure out if man ever makes wisdom a sole pursuit, but current life-cycle researchers have surprised us with a more balanced view of our predicament. Youth regards anyone past thirty as being over the hill. Adults used to think of their middle years as one long stretch of time, uninterrupted by highs and lows. No change or developments were perceived other than growing old. This rather boring concept has been challenged by life-cycles researchers during the Seventies. They told us that all of life is a series of stages. We journey through periods of stability, which are regularly interrupted by painful transitions.

Midway in life's journey I was made aware,
I had strayed into a deep, dark forest —
and I could not find the right path anywhere.

(Dante)

UPHEAVALS AND TRANSITIONS

Whenever we enter a new cycle or decade (give or take a couple of years), we collide with an identity crisis. It seems that we are not accepting the fact of growing older magnimoniously. Trying to hold on to the last glow of youth, or middle age, we fight turning forty or fifty, and these inner upheavals might not even occur on a conscious level. We pretend that aging does not matter and wonder why we are irritable and depressed.

The age-30 transition may be tinged with regret for lost youth, until anticipation of what lies ahead tempts us to better attitudes. The age-40 transition finds us vulnerable and wrestling with responsibility tangles. Eventually we swing over to the belief that life begins at forty after all. The age-50 transition often hits us with painful intensity and causes a period of retreat and depression. After fighting the idea of turning fifty, people discover to their own amazement that they might be half a century old, but still feel as young as ever. They are then swept into a culmination of middle adulthood. After passing each of these painful transitions, the identity crisis diminishes. We adjust to the new cycle and settle into a new phase of heightened awareness.

Lessons In Growing
THE GROWTH PERSON

Life-cycle research offers a fascinating concept of change and growth. We do not remain static, but acquire different likes and dislikes, discard old habits and find new interests. We separate from people with whom we shared decades of intimacy. Always, new crises must be overcome and new challenges met. The result can only be an ever-widening understanding of life, other people and ourselves. At fifty, our youthful image seems like that of another person. At seventy, we have once again entirely different priorities. Growth includes the privilege of changing our mind, as our perspective comes from an increasingly elevated position. In the end we should have mastered the hardest task of all: we not only know ourselves, but we have made peace with a world that falls far short from our youthful expectations. We have gained compassion because our own outlook has been subjected to the full swing of the pendulum:

88

COMPARISON

** Can you identify with the emotions and attitudes expressed during the various stages of life?*

1. YOUTH
2. MIDDLE AGE
3. OLD AGE

- ☐ 1. I'm discontent with the established order.
- ☐ 2. I support order and the establishment.
- ☐ 3. I'm resigned to the state of affairs.

- ☐ 1. I believe in progress and innovation.
- ☐ 2. I follow accepted routines.
- ☐ 3. We should get back to old traditions.

- ☐ 1. I act on impulse.
- ☐ 2. I think before I act.
- ☐ 3. I rest before I think.

- ☐ 1. I relish excitement.
- ☐ 2. I save excitement for peak experiences.
- ☐ 3. I avoid taxing excitement.

- ☐ 1. I live for the future.
- ☐ 2. I live for the here and now.
- ☐ 3. I draw from the past, hope for the future, and make the best of today.

THE PERIODS OF
STABILITY

Focusing on duality and the pendulum of choice, what options do we have to turn each cycle to advantage? What kind of conflicts do we encounter in each developmental stage? Most importantly: **How can we accomplish inner growth within the highly competitive set-up of society?**

YOUNG ADULT WORLD
20-30

After breaking away from the family and a time of emotional insecurity, the forming of goals and the process of expansion begin. An adjustment to the demands of society sets in and the rebelliousness of youth subsides. The establishment beckons with its options: the working world in America is made for the young with their promise of being eager and adaptable. Advancement is best accomplished from the ground floor up and by learning the inside-out operations of the home base. Bursting with zest and vigor, the youthful employee tries to secure a platform from which he can compete.

In shaping their private lives, young couples are unincumbered by the traditions which used to divide the man's world from the woman's domain. Boundaries are no longer sharply defined and the traditional family pattern with father as provider and mother taking care of the children does no longer constitute the norm. Women are functioning as additional wage earners — some by inner drive, others by necessity. They are united in their desire to not merely bring home a paycheck, but find fulfillment or make a contribution in their work. This means that husbands and wives are no longer out of touch — their worlds have become interrelated. The wife can identify with the demands and routines of earning a living. She has the opportunity to prove her own ingenuity and competence. The husband in turn no longer finds it beneath his dignity to extend a helping hand with household chores and child-rearing duties. Modern marriages have the chance to develop into a true partnership: working together for the mutual benefit... and sharing, rather than dividing, their interests at home and at work. Couples who know how to communicate and give one another **support** may face the growth process of the coming cycles from a new vantage point: that of increased respect for the partner's duties. Sociologists and psychologists have not yet tabulated statistics. Is it a better way than the family concept of the old? According to individual maturity, the modern husband-wife-relationship should prove to be a blessing, rather than a burden.

Within these new developments, the 20-to-30 age is a peak time of being self-motivated for men and women, trying to build a foundation for their future. Youthful narcissism, however, still lingers on. We are intensely involved in getting to know ourselves. What are our needs? What are our priorities and have we developed a value system? How many sacrifices are we willing to make for love? Gradually we gain assurance of our own reactions and narcissism is replaced with self-confidence and a broadening view of our responsibilities.

SETTLING INTO MID-LIFE
30-40

The pendulum no longer swings to youthful extremes; we are settling down into the I-LIKE-MYSELF attitude as we are gaining confidence in our abilities. But the pull of the opposites is still strong. While this decade brings peak experiences with the rewards of parentage, the marriage itself becomes vulnerable through familiarity and fatigue. The self-improver and the no-growth person discover their basic incompatibility. From here on, they will continue to drift apart, unless the no-growth-partner has a change of heart.

Energies are extended towards material security; the struggle is still uphill and success is a tantalizing hope. The striving to achieve ambitions turns into a threat — we are vulnerable to the temptation of over-achieving. Our on-the-job behavior becomes conditioned by the professional environment which may be one of superficial values. The tactics of manipulation are often masked by a surface politeness; courtesy serves as a calculated facade demanded by employers. Our at-work personality might be cool and in command — not at all consistent with how we feel.

This decade is decisive for the entire future. Have we found the atmosphere that fills our inner needs and is it in tune with our personal values? Or must we constantly prove our worth as over-achievers? Exposed to such conflicts, it is wise to contemplate alternatives, since a good part of the working years still lie ahead. Questioning the double standards should motivate us to set new goals, no matter if they are long-range.

MID-LIFE HIGHS AND LOWS
40-50

This decade begins with a life-starts-at-forty attitude and ends with the half-century-crisis. During the intervening period of stability, middle-agers have established lasting values and a stable pattern of life, which includes the accu-

92

mulation of certain material assets. Upon their grown-up children leaving home, husband and wife must face the challenge of expanding their intellectual activities. Physically still young and vigorous, they might utilize the opportunity to realize old desires, such as traveling, or getting involved in hobbies. Best of all, they feel comfortable with who they are. The I-TRUST-MYSELF attitude is a welcome sign of maturity. The own image is that of a growth-person. Free from the last trace of narcissism, there is no need to seek identity through others (a parent, a mate or an admired peer). How fortunate we are! In previous centuries, forty-plus people looked, felt and behaved old. Today, we consider this decade as a highlight time... with no limits on options. Whether our decisions are wise or foolish — we feel free to live any way we like.

Sometimes during this decade we notice a change in our attitudes towards work — a growing detachment can be observed. It is unlikely that we will win top prizes, but such desire no longer carries much importance; there are other, personal things that interest us more. We have the feeling that inner growth should no longer be delayed because we have become conscious of the fact that time is fleeting.

CULMINATION
50-60

During the pre-retirement years we look back over the decades and realize that each cycle had its own beauties — a thought designed to stimulate the acceptance of what is to come. Europeans have long felt at home with accepting the aging process gracefully. They slip into each developmental stage with less trauma and emotional insecurity than Americans. They retain their skepticism about the youth cult and feel comfortable with getting older to the point of being lighthearted about the changing appearance. They are neither obsessed with losing the weight that cushions middle age, nor with rinsing the grey out of the hair. Elders have always held a respected position as givers of support and advice.

RETIREMENT
65+

Youth, middle age and old age comprise the whole of life, residing at different points of the cycle. The generations may love, enjoy and inspire one another in partnership. Sharing emotional awareness of the human seasons enriches the quality of our existence at any age.

Old people are endowed with a special affinity for children, and they are drawn to animals, nature, and the simple joys. If retirement is coupled with good health, it does offer an opportunity for which we have waited a long time. We have earned the privilege to awaken each morning and ask ourselves: What will give me pleasure today? Our time is our own, to be used and squandered in splendor. No one need to feel guilty, for a contented person serves as inspiration for those who fret away their precious hours. Now we are reaping the benefits of life-long self-improvement!

POSITIVE CHOICES

The concept of life-cycles — being interrupted by periods of transition — equals the pendulum principle of strife and reconciliation. Antagonistic opposites need one another to be complete, or to produce something new. If our personal cycles are subject to the laws of duality, then they must have a similar purpose.

The purpose of duality is to present us with a clear choice — experiencing the negative helps us to knowingly embrace the positive. In the same manner, each transition or time of conflict is followed by renewed vigor and increased maturity. We move from restlessness to stability, from doubt to understanding. **Only the gaining of wisdom can be the purpose of our stop-and-go journey. As a growth-person, we consciously absorb lessons from each cycle.**

It seems that the task of choosing the positive remains with us — especially in old age. Forced to accept the weakness of the body, we may still cultivate the strength of the mind. Having slowed down in our activities, we are compensated by the peace and tranquility which we find in the comfort zone. The better we utilize our years, the richer unfolds our storehouse of memories. At last we understand the magnitude of it all: the pendulum swings from chance to purpose and from error to truth, forcing us to experience the whole of life. We could not run through it all at an unrelenting speed. We need to pause, catch our breath, review our errors and try again with increased confidence.

CHAPTER 7

A DIALOGUE WITH YOUTH

If the young commit a fault,
it is always on the side of
excess and exaggeration.
(Aristotle)

I can regulate the pendulum-swings
to the extremes, and build a good,
workable philosophy of life.

In time,
Even youth grows old.
(Oriental Proverb)

In a recent survey, a majority of students stressed the importance of a **philosophy of life** – but the teenagers could only name such obvious things as having a satisfying job, raising a family and being a good citizen. If we seek the opportunity for an occasional heart-to-heart talk with young persons we like, what are the things we can mention to reinforce values?

*Conversation between
an ADULT and a YOUTH:*

ADULT: I'm reading here that today's multi-billion-dollar education is only producing apathy and orneriness. What are you youngsters doing to deserve this?

YOUTH: Wait, let me read something to you: "Young people have bad manners, contempt for authority, disrespect for their elders. Children nowadays are tyrants." Who do you think said that?

A: It doesn't sound like Dr. Spock. Tell me.

Y: It was Socrates. So you see, adults have always been downgrading youth. Why?

A: Perhaps because we envy you.

Y: Now I know that you're pulling my leg.

A: Not really. Haven't you noticed how sentimental adults get when they talk about their youth? They loved the exuberance and vitality and those starry-eyed expectations. The colors of youth are bright and vibrant. Later, the greys and blacks fill in and the picture gets more realistic.

Y: Then why don't you go on feeling that way?

A: Because it's too exasperating in the long run. Ecstasy one moment... and brooding the next. From being irritated to high excitement... everything is exaggerated into a sensation. Don't forget, when grown-ups say: "Ah, to be young again!", they quickly add: "But only if I had the wisdom of today..."

Y: Big deal.

A: Yes it is. It's the only thing we get in the bargain. But it is so important to us that we wouldn't trade it back.

Y: Why wouldn't you?

A: Let me think of a few reasons. You like the fact that you don't fall for flattery, don't get taken in anymore and you've learned to say NO to unreasonable demands; there's no need to be on the alert all the time. You know for sure that someone won't like what you wear or say, but it doesn't matter. On the other side, a few good people continue to love you even when you're feisty and ornery, and that more than evens things out. You like yourself, because you know that no matter how good a job you perform, others can do it better or worse, so you accept your own efforts. What else? It's good to keep happily busy even on a rainy Sunday afternoon. It's a relief to look at problems and decide which one to worry about tomorrow and which one to forget right now. And no matter how old you get, it's by far not old enough to know it all.

Y: That's interesting; it doesn't sound too bad to learn

any of these things. Does that mean that you simply get a lot of answers as time goes by?

A: Exactly. You get them with and without asking questions. By reading, by observing and by experiencing — all sorts of ways.

Y: But you can't tell me that everybody learns from other people's experiences?

A: Everybody should, but some people don't allow the impact of the answers — which are really solutions to problems — to sink in. They look at life as a trial-and-error-playpen.

Y: How do you see it?

A: If your common sense prevails, as a STOP-THINK-CORRECT school. The beauty of being a self-improver is that you merely have to WANT to be one, and then it comes gradually, without a big fuss or effort. When you make a mistake and don't like the result, you merely take a mental note to do better next time.

Y : You make it sound so simple.

A: Well, that seems to be another lesson I learned. The simpler you keep it, the better are your chances to remember. You know, a wise person once said: "When I wake up in the morning I have two choices – to be satisfied or dissatisfied. I choose satisfaction." You can't put it more simply or effectively.

Y : I can't argue with you on that. But how can one stay satisfied? In the first place, I'm simply not able to control my mood swings.

A: Oh yes, you can. You can hold a little conversation with yourself and figure out why you have every reason in the world to be content — and then YOU are the one to turn off the negative thoughts. Who else is going to do it for you?

Y: Are you satisfied 24 hours a day ?

A: Heaven forbid. But I'm succeeding more and more to keep the pendulum from swinging to extremes, and I consider that quite an accomplishment. When I find my mind endlessly spinning around the same aggravating thoughts like a stuck record, I switch off mentally. I turn to something that gives me pleasure. You know, the week only has 168 hours — nobody gets any more. Some people manage to make themselves thoroughly miserable during their waking hours, while others enjoy themselves to the best of their abilities.

Y: O.K., so you said that when you're dissatisfied, you switch off the negative thoughts by doing something you like. I can see that. When I'm in a bum mood, I walk my dogs in the park and it really gets my mind off my problems. But you haven't told me how to STAY satisfied.

A: Ah, I wish I could hand you a magic potion. You can beautify your exterior to a certain degree and obtain a lasting effect. For example, plastic surgery can correct a poor feature for the rest of a person's life. No more effort needed. But to beautify your interior and have a lasting effect? How does that work? You have to STOP - THINK - CORRECT time and again. Gradually, the pendulum does not swing to extremes any more. The periods of dissatisfaction become shorter, because you understand the futility of it and you stay satisfied longer.

Y: Is that the best you can do?

A: It doesn't sound half bad, if you weigh the alternatives. It sounds even better considering that in adulthood your expectations are far more realistic. How can you be disappointed if you don't expect the impossible? You also stop going out of your way looking for trouble.

Y: Let me see if I got this straight.   An adult.... wait a minute, that's a wrong premise already....

A: .. My favorite term is: a self-improver - -

Y: - - A self-improver knows he has only so many waking hours a week and tries to make the most of them. I suppose your point is not to worry needlessly, but if you absolutely can't help it, then get off the dead-end-street and onto another road. And if you don't expect a trip to the amusement park to be the greatest experience of your life, you're going to enjoy it more. Is that what you're saying?

A: I am proud of you. Doesn't it make sense?

Y: I guess so. But I really have to think about it.

A: Fair enough. Now, don't be too hard on yourself, because we are not talking about solving all of your life's problems with one handy solution — obviously, that would be impossible. We are merely considering choices, trying to find the best attitude. As you put it so nicely: if you do turn away from the dead-end-road whenever you have the choice, you can look forward to a real pleasant surprise.

Y: You just said a minute ago that one shouldn't expect too much.

A: It sounds confusing, but you mentioned the right word. There's a world of difference between expecting too much... while hoping for the best. Expecting too much means making yourself vulnerable to disappointment. And hoping for the best? Thank God, that comes naturally to all of us.

Y: What if I don't have a clear-cut choice?

A: Then you make a compromise and try to be satisfied.

Y: Is that where the disappointment comes in which you mentioned a couple of times?

A: Exactly.

Y: But who wants to learn through disappointment?

A: Nobody. But again, you do best to consider choices. Are you going to become bitter and angry? That's absolutely natural. But are you going to stay frustrated and waste your time fretting? You can ask yourself what went wrong and try to learn from the experience.

Y: You can STOP - THINK - CORRECT.

A: I told you before, I am really proud of you. And I am enjoying this conversation. Tell me something — didn't you fail to make the team last year?

Y: You don't forget a thing.

A: What happened then?

Y: Well, I made it this year.

A: Why?

Y: Because I tried harder.

A: Right. Remember how disappointed you were at first? But you got over your ill feelings and practiced more seriously. You tried harder! These three words contain a lot of wisdom. Remember them.

Y: There are so many things you seem to want me to remember. I don't think I can do it.

A: You couldn't, I agree with you. And it's not the object. I'm just being a good gardener right now.

Y: Now, how am I to understand that?

A: Many years ago, I attended a lecture given by a truly wise man. He talked a lot about "planting seed thoughts" and I have never forgotten it because it really rang a bell in my mind. How often did my mother give me good advice? I didn't pay the least attention to it. Years later I would come to her and say: "Hey, Mom, listen to what I just discovered!" She would just smile. But one day, she said to me: "Don't you remember? I told you the same thing years ago."

Y: I can relate to that.

A: Yes. That's exactly what I mean about being a self-improver without making a big deal of it. Simply being open to seed thoughts is really a beautiful thing. Come to think of it, isn't that what youth is all about? At no other time in life are so many impressions gathered. Later, you will learn to separate the chaff from the wheat — you are going to discriminate. But in youth, you simply have a roaming mind and take in everything you can. The more consciously you do it, the more you will get out of life. Now and later.

Y: I like that a lot. Do you still call it learning?

A: I personally do, but I happen to think that learning is fun. It makes you feel good. It gives you knowledge, self-assurance and is the best way towards self-approval.

Y: Is that so important?

A: It's a priority. It's - -

Y: - Another thing you just happened to learn.

A: O.K., wise guy. Now you're making fun of me. I had a hunch that the idea of patiently waiting for seed thoughts to blossom would sound somewhat strange to an impatient youth.

Y: No, I'm really interested in hearing more about self-approval.

A: It simply means to like yourself.

Y: I gather that. But it's the last thing I expected you to say. Doesn't it seem rather selfish? Or conceited?

A: Not in the least. The self-improver who likes himself is the opposite of the self-indulger who expects other people to Take-Me—As—I—Am because he can't be expected to correct his hang-ups. The conceited person harbors the illusion that he is better than others.

Y: I know the types. Tell me more about your self-improvers.

A: I see them as the average nice people whom you meet all the time. They have neither inferiority nor superiority complexes because they view the world and themselves in perspective. They know their place and their status in life and they're satisfied with it. They accept themselves for what they are because they try to do the best they can under the circumstances.

Y: But I'm always worried about correcting my mistakes.

A: Hey, you are going to be a terrific self-improver! Admitting faults is overcoming one of the biggest hurdles. But I wouldn't be surprised if you are overly critical. A number of your shortcomings might even be imagined. For the moment, I would say — don't go out of your way looking for faults; there is a right time for everything. In youth you may rely on your parents to teach you values, such as knowing the difference between right and wrong. I think that's enough to handle. Your job right now is to get to know and like yourself and become a whole person.

Y: Sounds better than I expected. I thought that getting to know oneself is an ordeal. You make it sound like fun.

A: It's like digging for treasures, and youth loves discoveries. You can rest assured that you will find more hidden jewels than anticipated.

Y: Are you trying to build my self-confidence?

A: Of course. That's one aspect where adults can really be of help. Let me give you another reason for liking yourself, which should be important to you right now. How often are you persuaded to do something against your beliefs? How often do you give in to manipulation, suppressing your better instincts?

Y: You are right. I don't like this to happen.

A: As soon as your self-confidence rests securely, you can stop the everybody-is-doing-it fallacy.

Y: I thought we are supposed to conform? Shouldn't we fit in with society?

A: Of course. Friendship and fellowship give pleasure and fill our basic needs. We must be involved and share. But we must also check up on society's value system. Do you approve it? Does it coincide with your own inclinations? Society has been wrong as often as it proved to be right. If your friends get the sudden urge to behave extremely foolish, why go along? You are better off to excuse yourself and step aside. It's strange, but people don't dislike you for knowing your own mind. Generally, they rather respect you for it.

Y: I read a book on learning how to say no. It impressed me - what do you think?

A: It teaches the mechanics of untangling yourself from unwelcome situations. Making up your own mind — knowing what you want — saying no — resisting the pressure to conform at the wrong time.... this all has to do with feeling comfortable with yourself. You are now prepared to handle unpleasant confrontations.

Y: Won't I feel lonely if I don't conform?

A: You always find like-minded friends. One true friendship based on mutual respect is better than pleasing a crowd. Youth is a time of paradox — you may feel lonely and abandoned in the midst of companions. It has to do with needing approval from parents, teachers, classmates, and friends... we are so unsure of ourselves that we need far more verbal reassurances than we ever receive.

Y: You mean this won't change until - -

A: - - until you become satisfied with the assurance and moral support you get from yourself. It takes time. And patience. And experience — all the things which youth tends to regard as unimportant.

Y: And then I'll like myself, I suppose?

A: You'll like yourself very well indeed. You will have have earned it.

Y: One last question. Any advice on how to make the best choices?

A: For sure. Always consider the consequences!

xxxxxxxxxxxxxxxxxxxxxxxxxxxxxxxxxxxxxxxxxxxxxxxxxxxxxxxxxxxxxxx

CHAPTER 8

THE LURE OF MARRIAGE

*Only when a human being is happily
married to himself, is he fit
for married life to someone else.
(Novalis)*

I can best contribute to a happy union
by living in my comfort zone.

We hope to find a reserved seat next to the fireplace that keeps us warm, secure and protected. We want to share this cozy niche with someone who is so close to us that the glow of love soothes our whole being with a contentment surpassing all other experiences. It is love that we long for, to give and receive and to fill our every action with meaning. But one day the mood of utter contentment passes and the flames eventually burn down. We cannot chisel that moment of hope and expectation in stone... we have to be satisfied with the realization that emotions and unions can be as temporary as the seasons, and that only the memory remains. Since the days of living in caves, marriage has been the most popular form of togetherness. But its popularity does not guarantee everlasting bliss.

> The kindest and the happiest pair
> will find occasion to forbear;
> and something, every day they live
> to pity... and perhaps forgive.
> (William Cowper)

Evidently — judging by the divorce rate — it is getting increasingly harder to forbear, pity and forgive. Marriage as an institution suffers under the eternal contradiction between expectation and reality. An acquaintance wrote a little verse after her third divorce that sums up her change of heart:

YOU FOOLED ME

> I thought your hair was golden,
> while it is mousey-grey.
> I thought you were mysterious,
> but you have feet of clay.
> I saw you as philosopher
> with feelings running deep -
> but now, alas, you seem to me
> a good-for-nothing creep.

READY FOR MARRIAGE?

Once upon a time, so went the American fairy tale, charming girl meets ambitious boy, both fall in love at first sight, the delighted families provide a lavish wedding and the young couple lives happily ever after.

Today, few expect to find a virgin partner, romance is discredited, live-in relationships are in vogue along with such things as making contracts, securing rights and suing for palimony. Times are a-changing. Now you can breathe free and easy knowing that you are allowed "to be your own person". You can have a child if you want to, but you don't have to get married if it doesn't please you. In every sense and fashion you may opt for your personal choices and it will help you to consider the consequences beforehand. Opinionated types will question all or most of these developments. But — in a country that cherishes freedom above all else — they allow the individual to pursue a desired life-style. Now that you don't need to rush into marriage to be socially acceptable, to advance in your job or please your family, take your time and think about it.

If two wouldn't have to
live together, marriage
would be wonderful!

*   *Are you the marrying type?*

☐   To me, living alone is definitely a negative choice. I want a lasting partnership. I am the marrying type.

☐   I believe living alone is a marvelous opportunity for growth, but I see it as a transition period. I prefer marriage, but I'd make the best of either situation.

☐   I love pursuing my priorities and I don't care for around—the—clock companionship. I believe in being independent. I am born to live alone.

Your choices are clear if you are the live-alone or the marrying type. Go ahead, set your goals, pursue them and make them work. If you have no clear-cut, definite preference, let life come to you. Have faith that the right option will present itself and in the meantime don't wait and postpone living — fill your time with all the activities you enjoy.

KNOW YOUR INCLINATIONS:

*   If you are contemplating marriage, chances arc that you have a lot to learn about your partner. But how well do you know yourself?

☐   I would appreciate the opportunity to enhance a mate's happiness. I enjoy taking care of someone.

☐   I derive pleasure in sharing my home and discussing the events of the day.

☐   I believe that marriage and family are worthy purposes to life's plan.

☐   I am the motherly/fatherly type and want to raise children.

☐   I like to devote my energies to my family's welfare.

If you answer these questions in the affirmative, you should look for the compatible partner you deserve.

KNOW YOUR TALENTS

*   Perhaps you have visions of becoming a famous musician, singer, writer or artist? Will this hope fade... or turn into a powerful drive?

- ☐   Yes, I have a strong drive to
      develop my talents.

- ☐   I need to seek opportunities
      to prove myself.

- ☐   I would feel a void giving up
      my ambitions.

If you answer these questions in the affirmative, you should carefully consider the preferences of your future mate. A non-supportive partner, whose inclinations differ from yours, would interfere with your needs and view them as a threat. A giving and enthusiastic partner would set the atmosphere to support and enhance your ambitions, helping you to realize your goals.

KNOW YOUR GOALS:

*   You might have strong motivations (such as travel, money, or career goals) that have to do with proving yourself or fulfilling a dream.

- ☐   Do I have goals that I would like to realize before getting maried?

- ☐   Do I dream of adventures that need to be fulfilled before settling down?

☐	Do I want to save money for a purpose that is important to me?

☐	Would I be satisfied putting the demands of marriage first?

Ask yourself, would your goals interfere with your marriage? Or could you pursue them even better with an understanding partner? You either need more time alone to satisfy your adventuresome spirit... or you need to realize these desires in partnership with a mate who shares your inclinations - otherwise you may think about things left undone for the rest of your life.

*	You should develop your talents and work for your goals.
*	You should cultivate your self-reliance.
*	You should realize your ambitions.
But what are your priorities?

Would your drives bring on conflicts? Would they threaten your marriage? Would their denial cause you unhappiness? Should you possibly delay marriage until you feel secure about your ambitions?

Thinking about these choices
will help you to choose wisely.

Society was in the habit of discrediting the single person's motivations. Don't feel there is something wrong, if you have a persistent dream that excludes being married. You need not apologize for not falling into the norm - not even to yourself. Contributions to humanity can be made from whatever vantage point you prefer.

MAKING MARRIAGE WORK

In the U.S., and prior to recent developments, marriage had always been romanticized as the end of wish fulfillment and the beginning of contentment—forever. Other countries have generally retained a more skeptical view of matrimony as an institution.... these are some of their proverbs:

* Before going to sea... say a prayer,
  before going to war... say two,
  before getting married... say three.   POLISH

* Marriage is the only evil that
  man anticipates with prayer.   GREEK

* Marry in haste, repent at leisure.   ENGLISH

* When marrying or taking pills, it is best
  not to hesitate too much.   DUTCH

* Marriages are made in heaven
  but consummated on earth.   FRENCH

* Marriage is the opposite of fever:
  it starts with a heat rash
  and ends with a cold.   GERMAN

* Marriage is the tomb of love.   RUSSIAN

* If you marry at all, marry last year.   IRISH

The suspicions expressed in these proverbs indicate that marriage does not provide Instant—Bliss. The first and most important task for two people to live in the comfort zone is to learn to communicate.

COMMUNICATING

*   ***What are you really saying?***

☐   Were you just trying to pay me
a compliment?

☐   Did you offer an excuse?

☐   Or did you criticize me?

☐   Why did I mistake a compliment
for a criticism?

☐   Could you have expressed yourself
better?

☐   Or did I read something into your
message that was not intended?

If you are not sure that you understand your mate's words or needs — DON'T ASSUME.... ASK. If the answer does not make sense, ask again, but reword your question. Think of your partner as multi-dimensional and work through the various emotional layers. ASK because you simply want to understand.

*   ***What goes on in his mind?***

    *   He likes it.
    *   He doesn't like it.
    *   Why doesn't he like it?
    *   Are his objections valid?
    *   If they are valid to him,
        can they be good enough for me?

114

Needs encompass many dimensions. Emotions have to be satisfied. The intellect needs stimulation. Health care constitutes a vital need. Parents have to agree on a philosophy of education. Being willing to compromise in such matters as recreation, life-style and finances requires a lot of problem-solving. Wise partners establish their priorities. When situations come up where they would find it difficult to compromise, they discuss them in a loving spirit. And they agree to never argue over things of little consequence. You and your mate should know one another's needs as well as you know your own.

*   *Does your mate know about your potential mood swings? Can he help you to regulate them?*

☐   I am an even-tempered person with a need
     for privacy.
☐   When aggravated, I may withdraw and do
     not communicate.

☐   I am a trusting person and like to see the
     good in people.
☐   At times, I allow people to take advantage
     of me.

☐   I respond to a kind comment or encouragement.
☐   When I feel insecure, I need an undue amount
     of praise.

Couples who enjoy a mature relationship are aware of mood swings and allow one another privacy, or give an encouraging world, until the partner returns to the comfort zone.

MAKING MARRIAGE LAST

You love one another?
Well then, learn to make it last.
(Nietzsche)

FAMILIARITY

Enraptured by the intimacy of sharing body and soul, young lovers believe this ecstasy is a permanent pleasure. Unfortunately, the beauty of intimacy can also prove to be the enemy of love. The all—too—familiar becomes wearisome and the candle of romance flickers. This is the time when work and imagination are needed to rekindle the flame; happy love-making alone won't assure a good relationship outside the bedroom.

* ***Are you forming loving habit patterns?***

☐ Not taking anything for granted, we exchange compliments and praise.

☐ We treat one another with consideration.

☐ From time to time we create a festive atmosphere.

☐ We show appreciation to one another in imaginative ways.

Love can wither if endless expectations fall upon the mate. Lovers often expect the other person to make them happy and generate contentment. Erich Fromm observes in THE ART OF LOVING that most people expect to BE LOVED rather than to BE LOVING...

116

TROUBLESOME EXPECTATIONS

* ***Are your expectations realistic?***

☐   I expect my mate to love me more.

☐   I expect my mate to make me happy.

☐   My wishes should be considered first.

☐   I should not have to control my moods,
    but be accepted as I am.

Faults are thick
when love wears thin.
(James Howell)

FAULTFINDING

The blindfolds of romance are soon removed in the daily routine of buying on credit and paying bills. When the petty pressures accumulate, mates find it harder to sustain a charitable frame of mind. Inconsistencies are no longer charming, but annoying. An ill mood does not bring out the desire to offer comfort, but to leave home. The idealized hero deflates into an ordinary fellow who can't be taught to throw his clothes into the hamper. The smart young woman can't get it together to organize household chores. The pendulum begins to oscillate on the negative side and faultfinding becomes an explosive issue. This is the time to lovingly communicate that your relationship will not fall into disrepair.

TROUBLESOME ATTITUDES

☐ I slide into the TAKE—ME—AS—I—AM attitude.

☐ I play the IT'S•NOT—MY—FAULT-game.

☐ I make YOU—NEVER—LOVED—ME accusations.

☐ I retreat and become unreachable.

How do we prevent our beautiful love to be worn away by something as unbecoming as pettiness? We call upon the reasoning mind and employ the STOP—THINK—CORRECT healing process.

STOP

We are getting upset and must stop immediately!

THINK

Can we discuss this rationally?

CORRECT

I am admitting my fault and am ready to listen to your point of view.

PREVENT

Can we learn not to repeat the same mistakes?

118

THE COMFORT ZONE

To make marriage work, we have to extend the I-LIKE-MYSELF and the I-TRUST-MYSELF attitudes to our partners. We are not only in love with our mate, but like his qualities, opinions and values. We trust him to behave, not according to our personal advantage, but in harmony with his ethics. If they differ from our own point of view, we respect his judgment. People enjoy sharing company with a contented person — a chronic complainer or self-pitier will encounter difficulties in remaining lovable. Only self-approvers who know how to dwell in their own comfort zone can respect a partner's needs and be a support giver. In a wholesome relationship, mates are not so clingy-dependent that they leave the other no space. Neither do they behave so independently as if no consideration were owed. Rather, couples compromise at a point of happy balance. Two whole people form a stable relationship and are supportive of one another.

The Art of Interdependence

    1.   Being too dependent.
    2.   Being too independent.
*   *3.   Being interdependent.*

    1.   I depend on my mate for decisions.
    2.   I don't like advice.
*   3.   We discuss and settle mutual concerns amiably.

    1.   I depend on my mate for approval.
    2.   I am guided only by my own judgment.
*   3.   We validate each other's confidence and
        self-esteem.

1.   I derive stability from my mate.

2.   I only rely on myself.

*   3.   We trust and support one another.

POSITIVE CHOICES

Love can survive a winter's frost and blossom lovelier than before. It requires effort and the greater the effort.... the happier the union. If you have found a partner with whom you can share intimacy — you are lucky. If you can make it last — you are wise.

♥ ♥ ♥ ♥ ♥ ♥ ♥ ♥ ♥ ♥ ♥ ♥ ♥ ♥ ♥ ♥ ♥

CHAPTER 9

SURVIVING DIVORCE

*I am more and more convinced that our
happiness or unhappiness depends
far more on the way we meet the events
of life, than on the nature of those
events themselves.
(Alexander Humboldt)*

Realizing that there is a purpose to
the pendulum of duality, I can meet
my fate with strength and benefit from
my experiences.

Divorce falls into the category of major trauma! It shatters the well-being of the personality and uproots the way of life. It cannot be overcome by a brief retreat and a few hours of meditation, but requires a long, painful healing process. Divorce pushes the pendulum over to the negative extreme. And it plays havoc with the pairs of opposites: love may turn into hate... trust into doubt... innocence into cynicism. Is there still a purpose to duality? Can the sufferer believe that without pain there would be no growth? Does the failure of youth's sweet dreams carry the seed to a new fulfillment? Or must we view divorce as a totally negative experience? We find the answers to such unsettling questions in the pendulum principle of dual options.

THE CRISIS

Prior to the final break-up, one or both partners may have been unwilling to admit that the relationship was about to end. How could this happen? Where did love go wrong? Husband and wife remember the hopes and promises and they may struggle to keep illusions intact. Since incompatibility is seen as a personal failure, the denial of reality serves as a protective shield while going through a traumatic period of rationalizing and shifting blame.

When the divorce is accepted as inevitable, the process moves into a new phase — the transition has been made from denial to confusion... hurt... loss of identity and anger. Struggling to overcome negative feelings, the mind is rarely in a state to view the facts objectively or to abide by logic. It is natural to accuse the other person and be torn by resentments.

☐ My anger is unrestrained and turning
into bitterness.

- ☐ It prevents me from functioning wholesomely.

- ☐ I realize that my anger prolongs my suffering.

The anxiety/anger aftermath is normal, but prolonging the rationalizing stage may lead to depression. Accusations fan the fires of resentment. We give in to the instinct to lash out when hurt and to hate those whom we used to love.

- ☐ Am I angry because I was wronged?

- ☐ Or am I angry because I acted against my better judgment?

- ☐ Can I overcome hate, anger or resentment by my own better insights?

Sooner or later the self-improver will let anger dissipate and try to progress into the healing phase. Time works as the supreme healer, and it is good to move with it and not against its soothing effects. Forgiveness may well be difficult — but **forgetting** remains an absolute. Without releasing the painful memories, inner harmony cannot be found. And it rarely seems possible to strive for a happier future before exorcising the ghosts of the past.

- ☐ Can I transform my anger into forgiveness?

- ☐ Can I forgive my former partner... and myself?

- ☐ Can I do it by my own efforts or do I need professional help?

HEALING AND
REBUILDING

If you should experience this trauma, find a caring person whose judgment you trust. Verbalize your anger, work through it from all angles. and do not let your ego stand in the way of admitting shortcomings. If you can walk through your trauma objectively, you are on the road to emotional recovery. If you do not have the support of an intimate friend — who can furnish you with the information that your own frame of mind tends to overlook — then seek professional guidance. Individual counseling with a recommended expert or group therapy should help you to get on the other side of your negative emotions.

At first, working through anger and resentment leaves the newly divorced in an emotional limbo. Energies have been spent to eliminate the negative — now a time of retreat and regrouping is in order. Moving from suffering to healing has been a painful transition. At this stage, the self-improver is getting in touch with the inner reservoir of strength. It needs to be replenished by initiative. Do not get impatient if you cannot shift to the positive as forcefully as you had hoped.

Trust the power of your healing faculties and do not let loneliness tempt you to make comparisons; it has been said that memory is a curse as well as a blessing. I have a friend who copes with the problem of false sentimentality in a way that works well for her. Whenever she feels sorry for herself, she dates her ex-husband. After an excruciatingly boring, exhausting evening, she is reminded how frustrated she was with pettiness as a constant companionship.

124

How can you conquer loneliness? You walk away from
the conditions that cause it and develop better habits. Revi-
talize loneliness into a constructive solitude. That is vital for
the healing process.

- ☐ I have the option to create a PLACE that
     gives me a good feeling when I come home.

- ☐ I have the option to occupy my TIME
     creatively.

- ☐ I am seeking a new social circle for
     diversion and recreation.

- ☐ I must become a self-starter.

Sometimes we observe couples parting amiably and
with dignity. They go their separate ways; they agree to extend friendship in hours of need   and shield their children
from the traumatic effects.

But all too often, the marriage resembled a battle-
field and partners emerge from the ordeal much like wounded
soldiers. Still in a state of shock, they haven't been able to
survey the extent of the damage done to the body and the
psyche. They have to recover from a relationship where
hostility fermented into a routine and where communication
meant throwing insults at one another   in the manner of the
Lockhorn cartoons.

Divorce each partner to fall back on his strength
and face the challenge to build a new life. Knowing that the
worst is over, the sufferer rallies and regroups. The tangled
nervous system calms down and – released from the drive to
retaliate – the individual returns to the pleasure of behaving
civilized. It is time to rebuild. Can aloneness lead to a new,
positive goal orientation? Is it possible to live peacefully in
one's own company?

Solitude and companionship
should be allowed to take turns —
one cures the other.
(Lucius Seneca)

IDENTIFYING NEEDS

In this process of becoming wholesome, it is important to consider needs. Marriage partners have been conditioned to believe that a mate is needed for happiness. The other person is expected to provide confidence and support. Chances are that most young people exchanged dependency on parents with the state of being dependent on a mate — now the newly divorced have to become self-reliant problem—solvers. They have to rebuild self-esteem. **The best way to begin is to first identify... and then satisfy the inner needs:**

☐ Do I require solitude or companionship?

☐ Do I employ my hours of solitude as a stage of growth and preparation?

☐ Do I need intellectual—emotional attachments?

☐ Or would I prefer romantic— sexual relationships?

☐ Would I be happiest developing career potentials?

☐ Would it give me satisfaction to develop my talents?

☐ What can I do to stimulate the intellect?

To identify your needs and become a self-starter, examine your temperament, character, background, education and all other essentials. Make a list of what gives you joy, and then establish your priorities. Knowing your likes and dislikes, you are ready to investigate your options and set your goals. Grasp the opportunity to enrich your life with the numerous pleasurable stimulations that ingenious people in your city have made available. No longer relying on a partner for decisions, you are discovering how capable you are to act on your own. It inspires you with confidence and an uplifting sense of freedom. Let your enthusiasm to explore compel others to participate. It is important to supplement your newly found emotional autonomy with the warmth of friendship, to honor your needs for laughter and acceptance.

* *Staying in the Comfort Zone:*

☐ Do I have a few trusted friends to
whom I can turn for emotional support?

☐ Can I share experiences with someone
who cares?

☐ Am I able to reach out, drawing
strength from others?

☐ Am I taking the initiative to
meet like-minded people?

Hope does not die till the last breath;
it sustains us in our voyage through life.
(Rouchefoucauld)

POSITIVE GROWTH

Whether we are aware of it or not, hope resides eternally in the human heart. We can only be downcast for so long, and then we anticipate the end of the dark tunnel. We only need to be thrown a life-line and we grasp it fervently, to set our mind towards new horizons. Hope is a motivator of thought and actions, refusing to accept the finality of suffering. If we have been disappointed in one person... how can we possibly retreat from mankind? If it took us years to find out that expectations falter... why should we feel defeated? Are we not that much closer to realizing other desires? The hope which beckons on the positive side of the pendulum is so powerful that it wins out as inevitably as light follows darkness.

The hope that emerges after a time of sadness springs from the wells of a deeply rooted resilience. Our powers of discrimination have been sharpened. Rising to the better self starts out a new, positive cycle. And we realize with joy: the personality has been shaped and beautified — we have been transformed and gained strength. Accepting the perpetual process of becoming, we are eager to go forward with courage — to be involved and committed to life and growth.

Divorce occurs mostly between the ages of twenty-five to thirty-five: during a cycle of energy peak and vitality. The need to earn a living (and to support children) leaves little time to brood. The will to succeed in building a new life occupies the mind. Work and career take on a new importance; women who find themselves as the head of the household are accomplishing marvelous things. Forced by circumstances, they discover their talents at being enterprising and resourceful! They may combine motherhood with work... continue their education... transform old hobbies into a career; they are caught up in the pleasure of setting and working towards goals.

One young woman who always had the desire to write sat down one evening and gave a touching account about the trauma of changing goals. To fulfill the role of wife and mother was all she had ever wanted and she was frightened by having to prove herself in a new set of circumstances. The article was accepted by a metropolitan newspaper and she was asked to contribute a series. A publisher then offered her a contract for a book. This is a change of direction which she admittedly never would have tried without the bad luck of divorce.

One of life's most pleasant surprises is to experience first-hand that ill winds can indeed blow something good our way. Every so often, we are startled when a traumatic event turns out to be a blessing in disguise... leading to greater happiness than anticipated. Inevitably, divorce opens up the life-style and widens social horizons. Men and women need to share their feelings with others who understand. They join single—parents clubs or other groups where they mingle with like-minded, active and outgoing people. Exhilarated by the new options, the self-improver realizes that life is different now, but holds its own rewards.

> Do not try to light the ashes
> but build a new fire.
> (Oriental proverb)

DIVORCE:
LATER YEARS

Sometimes, divorce is mutually desired in later years. When grown-up children leave home, areas of common interest may have dwindled and there is little to share. If couples are walking different paths, then sex probably has also lost its glow. The thought of staying together for practical reasons holds no lure, and each partner prefers to begin anew.

Couples who feel enterprising enough to strike out once again on their own do not look upon age as a barrier, but display an adventuresome spirit. Living for the here and now, they are determined to enjoy each life cycle to the fullest.

> When the wife grows old
> the husband turns cold,
> he wants his wine in a new bottle.
>
> (Ancient Proverb)

"I feel young, vigorous, and ready to conquer the world... until I sit at the breakfast table and take a look at my wife. Why am I chained to an old woman?" The sentiments expressed in this letter are legion. How can the faithful housewife win the competition with the husband's worldwise young co-worker? And how does she survive the trauma of being abandoned at a time she should be harvesting the fruits of her labors? Unlike the widow who can cherish loving memories, she is haunted by a feeling of unworthiness.

If she would seek professional help, a good counselor would start with the most elementary rebuilding of the self-image. It is a long and painful task, and the healing process proceeds one step at a time. But once a breakthrough is reached the rewards can be gratifying. She finds a surging release in moving from dependence to self-reliance. For the first time in decades, she can discover her needs and develop her personality according to her own likes. She learns to be a self-starter and to take responsibility. At last, she is willing to admit that "he" didn't attract her anymore either. Let the young wife bolster his ego-needs — she has found better things to do. The trauma of rejection is replaced by the desire to make up for lost time and to enjoy life in a liberating set of circumstances. Depending on the own attitude, every story has the potential of a happy ending.

* *Considering the pendulum of choice, are
you appreciating the rewards of your
independence?*

☐ I am resourceful and investigate my
options.

☐ I am self-sufficient and rely on my
judgment.

☐ I appreciate making my own decisions.

☐ I am responsible for the demands of
daily living.

☐ I have the option to work towards
career goals.

☐ I don't need to account for my
actions to anyone!

POSITIVE CHOICES

Divorce is traumatic because people feel that they have failed at something they wanted very much. But it is encouraging to read about the nature of making mistakes: "Every failure is a step to success; every detection of what is false directs us toward what is true." wrote the English philosopher William Whewell. In that sense, each misfortune contains the seeds of a new fulfillment, if it is viewed as a growth experience. Only one real calamity can befall us — to give up. Rewards come to those who keep on trying.

□ □ □ □ □ □ □ □ □ ■ □ □ □ □ □ □ □ □ □ □

CHAPTER 10

MATURE ACTIVE YEARS

*Living begins when the eager
passions of youth have cooled.
(Proverb)*

I can survive crises and I can enjoy
the peaks of my creative years,
because I am still a growth-person.

In 1932 Walter B. Pitkin wrote a book which became an overnight sensation: "LIFE BEGINS AT FORTY." At long last, Victorian ground-rules were laid to rest. People shouldn't behave with the same polite restraint at ages 35 or 65. They shouldn't be satisfied to display an image of respectability merely to please convention. The book caused the pendulum of adulthood to swing from suppressing to exploring feelings because 40+ adults had longed to hear such an uplifting message. Their restless minds and hearts needed the confirmation that they should not view themselves as walking depositories of dignity, but as alive, eager and ever-active participants of change and growth.

Fifty years have gone by and the pendulum has once again swung over to the extreme. Our great-grandparents made themselves prematurely drab in fashion and life-style; they denied that adulthood blossoms in stages and that we do experience a blessed period of youthful maturity. Today's society would love to find the pill that stops aging altogether, and, short of such miraculous discovery, it resorts to potions, dyes, exercises and cosmetic surgery. The goal is to look young along with thinking young. Regardless of society's excesses, the individual has accepted the message of life beginning at forty as an invitation to keep the flames of adventure kindled.

FEELING GREAT
AT FORTY

The decade of being forty might well deserve the accolade of showering the horn of plenty upon us; it represents the summit of what we want and what we can be. Entering the decade, today's men and women can look more desirable than ever : a touch of maturity enhances still-youthfull appearance with the markings of character. Poise adds a luster which no young person has had the chance to refine,

alluring even the younger generation, if we recall the story of
The Graduate. But what is our most precious possession? We
cherish looks and vitality, yet we draw from our storehouse
of experience.

I—LIKE—MYSELF ATTITUDE

Contributing to the feeling of comfort, liking oneself
no longer beckons as a goal but is accepted as reality. Our
relationships are now conducted from the vantage point of
self-confidence. We've been manipulated enough that we no
longer tiptoe through rooms filled with strangers, desiring to
disappear through the floor. Our expectations of others have
shrunk to realistic proportions. As a result, we stand... not
a couple of notches below, but on even keel — looking who-
ever it is straight in the eye. We do respect other people's
priorities and are careful to select growth-persons as
friends.

Experience has nourished the fragile ego to normal
size. We have stopped being hyper-critical of self because
we use the mind as counselor. We are not haunted by approval
needs because we now take responsibility for making our
own decisions. Rejections no longer have a shattering effect,
because we've gained experience in problem-solving. What a
freedom comes from knowing that the capacities for mental
growth remain unimpaired!

Self-knowlege is another blessing that we simply
acquire over the years. Now we can judge in which situation
we prove reliable and stay away from the kind of trauma we
cannot readily handle. One happy day we discover that our
life runs smoothly and orderly because we have gained
command over our emotions. The pendulum is not allowed to
swing to the extremes at the slightest provocation and we
feel more comfortable that way. There are other benefits

that we appreciate, such as laughing at our eccentricities rather than getting uptight about them. And we continue to indulge in a few weaknesses because we don't want to become too saintly.

Have we mastered the art of contentment? At work, we no longer feel driven by the desire to set the world on fire: a reliable professionalism has been shaped by discipline. A certain satisfaction is derived from having lived through enough harrowing experiences to know that we haven't missed a thing. Hardly believing that the midpoint has been reached, we are determined to make the most of the present. Like Faust, who traded his immortal soul to Mephistopheles, we would like to implore the moment to linger on... because it is so beautiful.

STOCKTAKING

Even wisdom remains elusive and may succumb once again to the old antagonists: fear, doubt and worry. Approaching the half-century mark, few escape this crisis-time without a nagging panic. If we have gained maturity, what happened to the spirit of adventure? If we have married young, what are we missing? If we live alone, where does the understanding support-giver hide out? And can we anticipate no more than a placid round of daily routines? We think of lost opportunities and recall with a stab of pain the discrepancies between youthful dreams and mid-life realities. There is the joy of becoming a grandparent... intermixed with the painful recognition: "Am I really that old?" At work, bright young achievers pay eager attention to any sign of slippage.

It is time for stocktaking. We are told that the active years - the struggle for success - count for everything. We are taught that we prepare for old age by saving a nest egg and we've done our share. Now we wonder: perhaps more meaningful challenges are awaiting us in the last cycle of life? We look around and encounter oldsters who have turned into shadows of their former selves. Others sparkle with vitality. What is the secret? If the doer and the defeatist both enjoy physical health, can the difference be revealed solely in the attitudes? **Could this mean that we must remain growth-persons throughout all stages of life?** Self-improvers who begin preparing for old age in mid-life reap three benefits: they teach their children values — they help themselves — they develop compassion for their parents.

    ☐ Am I teaching my children to respect
      old age?

    ☐ Do I provide a good example in my
      own relationships to my elders?

    ☐ Am I aware that my elders thrive on love?

    ☐ Do I give them reassurances of being
      wanted and needed?

    ☐ Am I preparing mentally and
      spiritually for my later years?

    ☐ Do I exercise my mind, keeping it
      flexible and active?

Approaching the fifties, stocktaking includes a new challenge: to will away the torments assailing us whenever we glance into a mirror. It is time to quit the youth cult and to stop fighting the inevitable. "Worry about wrinkles? I've earned every one of them," said a grandmother far too involved in activities to have the time or inclination for a face lift. Remembering the wisdom of the Golden Mean, let us

dress youthfully as is suitable for our years, without trying
to turn the clock back. And let us be consoled by the fact
that we may still feel young, even if we definitely stopped
looking it.

REACHING FIFTY

The anguish of hitting fifty usually coincides with a
family-crisis-time. The grown children eagerly set out on
their own, while the parents are faced with the task to let go
gracefully. Mothers have to refurbish their way of life and
channel new aspirations. Fathers have to wrestle with
the belated sorrow that they can't make up for lost time. In
financial respect, a plateau has been reached, assets have accumulated and professional stability is anticipated. Life stretches
out like a deser t with few surprises in sight.

And now, when the gates should open for a more elevated view, people don't move on but fall into a state of
limbo. The goals have been accomplished. There are no more
problems to solve, no challenges to occupy the mind constructively. The good things are taken for granted and the achievers
succumb to the illusion that they have arrived and that there is
nothing more for which to strive

    ☐ Have I lost my ambitions?

    ☐ Am I restless... inactive...
       bored with the familiar?

    ☐ Am I at a loss what to do
       with myself?

    ☐ Do I take my blessings for granted?

*As we grow old
the beauty steals inward.
(Emerson)*

Inner growth is an ongoing process and so is goal-setting. There are no finite goals, since there is no end to BE—COMING. We can become nicer, more cultured, more loving, better educated, and as a result happier. We can become involved in a wide range of activites. We can become more interested and gain experience in whatever stimulates our fancy.

It is time to dust off our image as self-improver. During the decade of the forties we were conscious of our competence and maturity. We thought that we had automatically mastered the art of staying in our comfort zone. Being jolted into the fifty-plus crisis, we realize that times of painful transitions will always occur. It is up to our own effort to attain and maintain. To stay in the comfort zone we must still generate enthusiasm. We must still be self-motivators. Only our goals change, but never the task of goal-setting.

*   **What Road Should I Travel Now?**

☐   I realize that striving for goals is a continuing process.

☐   As soon as I reach a goal, I will set a new one.

☐   As I accomplish my professional amibitions, I will cultivate other interests.

☐   I don't want to drift into my old age, but remain in charge of my life.

The two chief goals are self-evident: to enjoy the here and now — and to prepare for the future. Why not embark onto the project with planning, study and care? At last you may reach back to the interests and talents that you've stored away since your youthful years. Can the old urge to be creative... to paint, write, sing, play an instrument... be re-awakened? Do you need solitude or companionship for stimulation? Join the millions of doers who can't find enough time for the things they love to pursue.

The seekers are interested in telepathy, dreams, astrology and the range of supernatural phenomena. **The amateur inventors** play with their latest electronic marvels as contentedly as the scientists in their laboratories. **Nature lovers** go camping, biking, trailing or boating for whole-scale recreation. **Sports enthusiasts** play any game imaginable for relaxation, diversion, exercise, competition or companionship. **The builders** saw, hammer, nail, glue, paste, mold, polish, stain and finish for hours on end. They use clay, wood, plastic, metals, glass, mosaics, ivory, whatever feels exquisite in their hands. Some imaginative and patient people build ships in bottles, dollhouses that are authentic right down to the patchwork quilts and bearskin rugs. Builders have created cities made of matches or tiny model cars with doors that open and close by using tweezers. Some builders spend thousands of hours with their creations, bent down uncomfortably yet having a wonderful time. **The collectors** patiently add one object to another until their drawers or bookshelves bulge with items that differ but slightly from one another. Yet it is knowing such difference that makes collecting worthwhile. **Modern homebodies** labor and fuss happily with every belonging and new acquisition. Adult education is made for them; they take courses in upholstery, ceramics or gardening. They become experts in such fields as furnishings, periods, styles, design and decoration. When it comes to food and drink, homebodies are connoisseurs and their knowledge can rival that of any professional. That's what working at a hobby is all about: having fun while gaining expertise. Another dimension is added to the personality.

This country abounds with doers courageous enough to change careers after the children have left home and mortgages are paid off. Whether as a housewife or as a worker, the expertise gained is put to use. Working in the fields of their interests, career-changers may start in their spare time hoping for eventual full-time earnings. But we need not contemplate such a drastic change of life-style. Merely by utilizing the talents which lay neglected during the hectic middle years, we are enriching the present and preparing admirably for the future.

FACING RETIREMENT

"Time's horses gallop down the lessening hill" and the stretch of road ahead shortens. Soon we have to live through another transition that will remove us from the arena and put us in the spectator seats. What are we going to do about the crisis? Is the pendulum going to swing to the discomfort zone, or can we meet the challenge head-on?

Throughout our adult years we participated in the competitive tasks because it was expected; we felt compelled to prove our competence. Now we are becoming conscious of a mellowing... a shifting of priorities. A gradual detachment from the entrapments is setting in... it may even ripen into delight at the prospect of retreat. We survived the rigorous routines of the workaday world and did our share, contributing whatever we could to the consumer society. We gave our full measure of discipline, even if at times we felt like exploding in frustration. Chances are that we had to overcompensate for each reward that we wrestled from a

140

demanding, competitive system. It doesn't seem so bad to
thumb our noses at all this hustle and bustle, feeling relieved
to step aside.

We let go of the clutches of materialism and the life-
style of acquisition. Considering alternatives, the thought of
involvement in causes holds a strong appeal. We have long
lost our missionary urge to reform the world, but now we are
contemplating the idea of losing self in the service of others.
If we cannot change injustice, maybe we can help relieve
suffering? The thought of contributing... of imparting
knowledge acquires a new meaning. As we are nearing
retirement we have one winner to carry us through the
crisis: **the healing force of our own attitudes.**

1. NEGATIVE ATTITUDES
2. **POSITIVE ATTITUDES**

1. I am afraid of old age.
2. **I have the faith and courage to meet
    any situation.**

1. I resign myself to feeling old.
2. **I take the best care of my physical
    and mental well-being.**

1. I don't like the world anymore.
2. **I am interested in current events but do
    not allow them to disturb me.**

1. I don't want to give up my life-style.
2. **Possessions are only temporary; I am not overly attracted to material things.**

1. I want to be in the center of things.
2. **I am learning to let go gracefully.**

1. I have only strength to take care of my needs.
2. **I husband my strength for joyous activities.**

1. I can't afford to be emotionally involved.
2. **I am grateful that I can still offer comfort and cheer to others.**

POSITIVE CHOICES

Preparing mentally for the spectator years, we realize that the very process of maturing ties us to life. Can we not contribute MORE, now that we have been strengthened by survival while learning to bend where we were unyielding before? What is this sudden surge of freedom that we are feeling?

* We have lost the sense of urgency to prove ourselves to a lot of people whose values do not coincide with our own.

* We no longer need to be loved by everybody.

*   While loving our family, we've come to cherish our aloneness.

*   We are freed from the drive to accumulate possessions as an outer sign of our inner worth.

*   Best of all, we are replacing fear with trust. We have learned to trust ourselves — why not trust fate as well?

Now we are practicing with the heart what we have long understood with the intellect: to live and let live. We are able to face reality squarely and flow with the stream. We've proven a good pupil; our attitudes are in tune with the wisdom of the sages. The detachment and inner freedom enables us to face old age gracefully.

ʃ ʃ ʃ ʃ ʃ ʃ ʃ ʃ ʃ ʃ ʃ ʃ ʃ ʃ ʃ ʃ ʃ ʃ ʃ

CHAPTER 11

THE SPECTATOR YEARS

Friend, find your inner strength,
Do not stand and rest;
We travel to the lights
Gleaming at the crest.
(Angelus Silesius)

I plan to remain loving and lovable
that I may enjoy the crest of my years
to the best of my abilities.

Come, my friends...
'Tis not too late
to seek a newer world.
(Tennyson)

We have traveled the longest part of the road and now we cherish our memories — they confirm that life was rich and diverse. Whenever efforts remained unrewarded, a pleasant surprise revived the spirit. Whenever disappointment hit hard, someone bequeathed a kindness unexpectedly. We have become reconciled with duality because we succeeded often enough at distilling the positive from traumatic learning experiences.

Inevitably, the twilight years are a time of saying good-bye. Our thoughts drift to the shores unknown, contemplating the words of Socrates that whatever lies beyond is fulfillment. Can there be an end to love? When we grieve for a kind-hearted human being whom we are losing, we want the best for him. And we hope that the best is a surging release, a new freedom of spirit and soul in a higher state of being. Seventy per cent of Americans believe in the survival after death, and the greater part of humanity has always taken for granted the idea of a better world beyond.

NEW HORIZONS

In spite of such outlook, the American attitude towards death was one of denial by pretense. Not verbalizing and dealing with the fears in their hearts there was no mention of death, only of "passing on" — no dead person, only a "dear departed." The terminally ill were shut off in isolation wards so that everybody else could be shielded from the pain and shock. The pendulum of an entire nation had swayed out of balance with reality.

The death-awareness movement of the late Seventies has brought about a remarkable change of consciousness. LIFE AFTER LIFE (1977), the surprise best-seller by DR.R. A.Moody, presents gripping case histories of patients near death or clinically pronounced dead. While exhibiting no respiration, heartbeat or brainwave activities, the dying patients get brief glimpses of another realm. After being revived, they stunned rescue workers by giving accurate accounts of the revival procedures. The readers of Dr. Moody's two books are fascinated by the descriptions of what it is like to die, and particularly by the unexpected happenings on the threshold of eternity.

Man has always wanted to believe that the soul is destined to live in the hereafter; since doubts constantly assail him, he longs for scientific proof. Twentieth-century science has convinced us of the **inadequacies of human perception.** Electricity could not be discovered by the five senses, yet its manifestations changed civilized life. The ultimate forces of reality are not at work in the things we perceive, but in the invisible waves of energies governing the universe.

It is entirely possible that the near-death phenomena (now being more widely researched) will one future day be regarded as a milestone. When Copernicus announced his then heretic notion that the earth revolved around the sun, he had no visible proof for his theories. When Columbus sailed upon his voyage, contemporaries could not possibly conceive that mankind had immeasurably advanced. The near-death occurrences may well lead to a new consciousness. Science may proceed to collect enough convincing data concluding that the human spirit can function independently of the physical body. What impact would an assured acceptance of a spiritual life have on us? Fear would be transformed into belief. Without fear, the mind would be far more open to the beauties and diversities of this earth. Knowing that we do not cease to be would inspire us to a grateful acceptance of our destiny on earth and to an overwhelming sense of purposefulness.

> Let me dream that love goes with us
> to the shores unknown.
> (Felicia Hemans)

WIDOWHOOD

What a difference would such a knowledge make to the surviving mate of a loving marriage? Grief would be transformed into the hope of a joyous reunion.

There are about ten million widows in the United States, and only about one per cent remarry. If you, dear reader, are a widow or widower, you might be frightened by the years of aloneness you are facing after a lifetime of sharing. How can you find strength? The wholesome qualities that allowed you to build a lasting marriage also serve in the time of loss. You were able to cope with the ebb and the flow of togetherness because you are a growth-person. This strength of character is not lost. The ability to view things in perspective worked in marriage and now these life-sustaining qualities will carry you through the trauma. Think of yourself as someone who gathers full momentum in times of crisis, using a fortitude that you did not even know you possess.

The recent strides made in reaching out a helping hand include the experience of widowhood; communities offer a variety of support-giving programs. No one need to carry grief alone, but may learn to manage it in a loving interchange with others who have been there. The comfort-givers may be relatives, friends or strangers with a desire to help because they understand. Accept the help available, and when the time comes, you may return the good deed to someone else in need.

THE HEALING PROCESS

Even such final loss as death can be met with opposing attitudes. Some survivors may remain locked in grief, others understand that time must run its course through a healing cycle. A beautiful attitude that often emerges can be gratitude. Loss brings about the realization that the whole of life was experienced in a life-time of sharing... and no human being can ask for more.

I   Realize that there are things that you cannot change and must learn to accept.

2   **Realize that there are things that only you can change.**

I.   I have lost my moral support and my confidence-giver.

2.   **I need to derive confidence from my own attitudes and activities.**

I.   I have lost the identity of being part of a team.

2.   **I must learn to be entirely self-reliant.**

1. I must face the fact that my loss is
    permanent.
2. **I must learn to be a self-starter
    and self-motivator.**

1. I have lost certain comforts that
    cannot be replaced.
2. **I must view my next cycle as a
    challenge and find a way to give it meaning.**

Give in to your memories; salute the fact that you loved one another the best you could. From the day of the wedding to the time of loss, marriage survived because you cared. You could be fretful and testy, because love makes people sensitive to differences, but in the end, making-up always won out. The caring and sharing was part of it all, and your book of marriage was written to the last page. Now you can remember with gratitude.

Life has not become meaningless because you are alone. The qualities that your mate loved are still there. The capabilities to feel deeply are still yours — you have become wiser. Do not isolate yourself in grief, but let others benefit from your compassion. Anticipate the day to feel deeply once again the joys of a world in bloom and harvest, with the rising and the setting sun, for you are part of the eternal cycle of creation.

‡ ‡ ‡ ‡ ‡ ‡ ‡ ‡ ‡ ‡ ‡ ‡ ‡ ‡ ‡

THE PROMISE

Age, even old age, should represent a culmination in the human being's evolution. We look upon the spectator years as a positive emotional experience. Such attitude is all the more vital, since the life span continues to expand. And the good news from medical authorities announce that living longer will also mean living better; old people greatly benefit from therapy and can live healthier than ever before. Gerontologists are discovering that our bodies and psyches are not automatically doomed with the onset of old age:

* Disease, formerly attributed to the aging process, is actually caused by various health factors.

* Senility may be brought about by malnutrition or even by psychological conditions and is subject to improvement.

* Slowed-down responses can be caused by over-anxiety and may be subject to improvement.

* Neurotic disorders decline (rather than increase) after the age of seventy.

STOCKTAKING

If we do become more enlightened as we grow older, you might ask, why are there so many dissatisfield elderly people whose world gets smaller and more self-centered? To keep on being loved, one must remain lovable. **We need to regulate the pendulum of our behavior no matter what the age.**

☐   I do not make it a habit to
complain about my health.

☐   I do not talk excessively
about the past.

☐   I am not critical of the younger
members of the family.

☐   I do not give advice unless
I am asked for it.

☐   I have learned to say NO when asked
for a favor that I do not wish to grant.

☐   I have an open mind and
am interested in others.

☐   I let it be known that I welcome
visitors and am a pleasant companion.

When a noble life grows old,
it does not reveal decline,
but enters the first days of immortality.
(Madame de Stael)

POSITIVE CHOICES

What uplifting experience it is to witness a family member growing ever more beautiful in character. Let us look upon such a person as an inspiration... for that is what we hope to become.

In a life-time of gaining wisdom, the members of the spectator generation have learned to judge the human condition with the clarity of a mirror polished to perfection. Now they hold but one desire: to live out the remaining years in harmony. But the forces of duality — the swings to the extremes which the elderly have learned to conquer — still disrupt the lives of their children.

Old people wish to reach out, to share the problem-solving knowledge so that their loved ones need not repeat the same mistakes of ambition or lust or vanity. But they realize that they can do little more than develop a charitable attitude towards the narcissism of the young.

In their relationships to the family, the TAKE-ME-AS-I-AM attitude has gained a meaning of humbleness: "I am weaker now, though I don't want to complain. Don't ask too much of me. Just love me without reserve, as I love you." Yet, a secret tie unites the old with the very young — the children and the elderly not only need one another, but communicate in a way from which the middle-agers have removed themselves. It has nothing to do with indulgence, but perhaps with the idea that children still... and grand-parents once again enjoy the telling of fairy tales.

So they retreat a little more into their own world, finding contentment with the faded and yellowed photos of yesterday and with the bonus pleasures of today — listening to music, a walk in the garden, the love of a pet. While their own world has become smaller, the capacity to enjoy little things has increased. Our beloved oldsters, it seems, have become the veteran gardeners they set out to be in their middle years, and have beautified their inner landscape.

Ɛ Ɛ Ɛ Ɛ Ɛ Ɛ Ɛ Ɛ Ɛ Ɛ Ɛ

CHAPTER 12

FROM ALONENESS TO SHARING

*Loneliness is but an opportunity
to cut adrift and find yourself.
(Anna Sharon Monroe)*

I have the choice to accept my aloneness
as a source of strength, while reaching out
in a loving and creative union with others.

I remember vividly my grandmother's charming tales of her youth. She was brought up in an isolated community in Europe where the harvest was plentiful and the farmers considered themselves well-to-do. In her reminiscences, grandmother painted the picture of a family-like unity that included every resident. She spoke of the commitment that people felt for one another. Everyone participated in celebrations and everyone extended a helping hand in times of distress. To be involved with one another's children and with the respected elders was a cherished tradition. No one felt a stranger and no one was lonely.

For thousands of years, the majority of this earth's population had lived a similar existence close to nature and to one another, In the United States, the closely knit relationships of our forefathers are depicted with nostalgia; we envy their sincere, open ways of relating to one another. Anyone familiar with such a life-style understands the gains and losses of progress. How lonely is the contemporary urban life in contrast to the feeling of belonging that people once shared.

CONTEMPORARY LONELINESS

Today, eighty per cent of the teenagers and seventy per cent of adult men and women suffer attacks of loneliness. What a paradox: we live closer together than ever before, but feel isolated and estranged. Crowded cities do not invite lasting attachments. The modern automated civilization, dependent on machines and technology, produces a regulated, functional and impersonal environment. Loneliness is felt as a depravation, we are missing the warm flow of sharing and knowing one another intimately. No one wants to turn back the clock to a condition of material hardship, but contemplating history we wonder why the pendulum of progress rarely settles for a midpoint of balance?

When the sorcerer's apprentice unleashed his master's demons, he discovered to his dismay that he could not control them. Somehow, while attaining wealth and power, the United States switched priorities. What a paradox — dedication to progress and the search for the good life denied us its most important qualities: human warmth and closeness. A holy man from India recently visited the United States and was asked to sum up his impressions: "America is a country where people are so lonely that they pay professionals large sums of money for the privilege of talking to someone." Is his assessment fair?

*People are lonely
because they build walls
instead of bridges.
(Joseph Fort Newton)*

COMMUNICATING

**   What are you really saying?*

At work, we rarely dare to confess emotions or reveal too much about the inner self. When attending meetings or group functions, we do not readily form friendships. Courteous generalities are substituted for a meaningful communication — we ask: "How are you?", but expect a brief, stereotype answer. We assure friends: "See you soon!" while we hardly find time to spend a refreshing hour of conversation with people we like. When socializing, people find it difficult to spontaneously communicate beyond superficialities.

GETTING TOGETHER?

A group of people,
Strangers when they meet,
And strangers when they leave.
And no one cares,
Really cares,
If you laugh or if you grieve.

A group of people
Standing or shuffling around,
Not knowing with whom to stay.
And no one cares,
Really cares
Whatever you have to say.

A group of strangers,
Each with a glass in hand,
And feeling ill at ease.
And no one cares,
Really cares,
They're just shooting the breeze.

A group of people,
Meeting from four to six,
For a time of idle chatter,
But whether you come
And when you go —
No one cares —
And it doesn't really matter.

PERSONAL LONELINESS

Loneliness has many shades. It may be caused by a person's inability to utilize time constructively or to form meaningful relationships. It may imply boredom, dissatisfaction and emptiness. Being in love may provoke a lonely feeling when understanding is lacking. The loss of someone with whom we shared intimacy may produce an overwhelming longing to recapture past happiness. Enforced isolation through illness or a negative change in our working conditions may provoke a crisis.

We are affected by sad news or the suffering of others — a melancholy mood lingers on and we feel the need to retreat. These tendencies are natural and we should not mistake them for a failure on our part. In order to overcome our trauma, we must understand its degree or intensity. We accept occasional loneliness without concern, as we accept the passing of clouds before the sun. If feeling lonely becomes a habit and develops into a medium trauma, we recognize the need to change for the positive. At all events we must prevent a major trauma: a chronic loneliness.

CHECKLIST

* *Is my loneliness... a 🗌 Minor — 🗌 Medium — or 🗌 Major Trauma?*

🗌 Do I feel lonely among my relatives?

🗌 Do I experience loneliness among my co-workers?

🗌 Am I overly intimidated?

☐ Do I readily retreat when among others?

☐ Am I feeling lonely to the point of
isolation?

☐ Do I give in to depression?

STOP

Getting in touch with the principle of free choice, we realize that we must be self-motivated to overcome loneliness.

THINK

☐ Is my melancholy caused by loneliness?

☐ Why am I allowing this to happen?

☐ What alternatives are available?

☐ Am I occupying my leisure-time
constructively?

☐ Am I filling my needs for love and
friendship?

CORRECT

The pendulum always offers at least two choices — even loneliness can be transformed into a growth experience. It is a stern teacher for it allows no further escape. Facing ourselves in silence, we can view the personality as an instrument that needs to be tuned. Am I lonely because I am out of harmony? Or am I experiencing a creative transition?

CREATIVE ALONENESS

There are times in life when we rise above our own expectations and accomplish more than we set out to do. Feeling elated, we are rewarded with evidence of the own worth — we have proven ourselves. To whom? To the inner self. Whatever the task may be, now the individual knows: "I can do it!". **We comprehend aloneness in an entirely positive sense; the Unique Me is the true source of strength.**

There is only one model of each human being — no one else thinks, feels or acts exactly like the other. Character traits ...talents...aspirations... they are as different as the will to mold them or the degree of determination. Our intelligence proves important in how we apply our gifts. The capacities of each person reveal inconsistencies; we may think of Albert Einstein, the genius who was said to be childlike innocent in a number of worldly matters. The unique personality consists of many complex components. Parents, teachers, friends may contribute to the unfolding, but the individual is the master of his ship. He must trust himself to be responsible for the direction and destination of the voyage.

Self-assurance stems from taking creative advantage of one's essential aloneness. We nourish dreams, master disappointments, bury hopes and set new goals. No one else shares these emotional involvements to the same degree. Others may offer encouragement, but whatever we do not handle ourselves remains undone. No one else can make major decisions for us — sometimes actions go against the better judgment of those who wish us well. Our essential aloneness accompanies us always — others love and support us, but we only walk hand in hand part of the way.

☐ I know the feeling of aloneness.

☐ I can cope with it, because I regard
    it as a common condition of humanity.

☐ I accept my individual uniqueness
    with humility.

☐ I realize that it constitutes my
    source of strength.

The mind that engages in creative
solitude acquires a lofty character.
(K.W. Humboldt)

THE REWARDS OF SOLITUDE

The creative person regards solitude as an enlightened state of being, providing the opportunity to look at things, listen to music, walk through nature or to be alone for heightened awareness. It is a time to...

pursue our interests —
search for ideas —
acquire knowledge —
discover fundamental truths —
feel inspired —
and be creative.

Solitude awakens the frame of mind which "bears it farther than the sun and stars..." (Emerson).

Accepting aloneness as a state of inspiration, we become aware of our role within an orderly functioning universe. Is each cycle of life guided by a higher destiny? Have we not encountered experiences which defy rational explanations?

In such enlightening moods we review our aspirations and commitments. Insights crystalize not while we are engaged in worldly activities, but in the silent hours of tuning in to the inner self. We progress from fearing aloneness to accepting it in a humble attitude. In the hours of creative aloneness, the seeking individual feels in harmony with the lonely silence of the universe. After a time of retreat, we experience a renewed eagerness for involvement.

- ☐ It is up to me to give my life meaning.

- ☐ I can transform loneliness into creative solitude.

- ☐ I regard it as an opportunity to enrich my life.

If you were never disillusioned you will never be enlightened.

THE PAIN AND PLEASURE OF SHARING

In childhood we depend on the immediate environment to fill our emotional needs and recognition of our essential aloneness is grasped early. We are being taught to keep responses in control..... not to reveal the anger, the regrets, the longings which disturb us. Realizing that certain actions cause consequences we learn to be on guard. There are intimacies we can share with mother, though we must learn when sharing is opportune. We can relate certain experiences to father, though we are not always sure if they will be understood. Relations with brothers and sisters fall victim to jealousies. These are the persons dearest to us, yet we suffer feelings of estrangement,

When we grow up and fall in love, we are so eager for affection without restraint that we throw our whole being into the adventure. Love is expected to accomplish the impossible: we nourish the illusion that it will reconcile duality, making us whole and complete. But only when two worlds blend in a meaningful closeness does working and living together generate happiness. As the pendulum of emotions swings between opposites, we must come to terms with the pain that companionships are imperfect. We continue to long for rapport, but no longer expect likemindedness — soul communicates with soul only in rare moments.

Lessons In Growing
THE GROWTH PERSON

So it is an illusion that we need a partnership such as marriage for GROWTH. The wholesome person learns no matter what the environment happens to be. Self-improvement should be pursued whatever the circumstances — the accomplishments sought in marriage may well be obtained when living alone:

* The growth process can be derived from
  our own inner resources.

* Involvement can be related to a task, a goal,
  anybody or anything that we care about.

* The attributes of giving and kindness can
  flow freely from our own make-up and
  become a natural behavior pattern.

* The pleasure of sharing things of beauty
  can be experienced with various likeable
  people.

162

Like love, self-enhancement requires effort. But unlike
love, there is no one else to blame in the event of failure.
No unpleasant surprises can throw us off balance. We might
as well learn to live with ourselves as happily as we can, for
there is one certainty: we are our own companions at all times.

☐   I try to overcome aloneness by reaching
     out and sharing.

☐   I do not place unrealistic expectations
     on others.

☐   Aloneness has taught me to be compassionate.

**We seek companionship in the hope
of improving our happiness.**

As a natural development, we progress from emotional
dependence on others to self-reliance. Asserting independence,
we gain confidence in our own judgment. Becoming mature,
we are at last ready to share our dreams and activities with
others to increase pleasure. Aloneness has taught us the
rewards of affection.

What do we gain? We share all that is constructive and
beautiful for our mutual benefit. We offer support in times
of distress. We are inspired by the contributions of talented
people. We learn from others about contemporary issues.
Sorting out the multiple contradictory experiences of life,
we help one another grow.

By reaching out beyond the immediate environment, we enrich our comfort zone. Exchanging fellowship, we select like-minded people with whom we touch a chord of mutuality. The purpose is to bring variety into our life and to participate in a diverse range of activities. To find enough time for what is truly meaningful, the creative person must learn to discriminate while filling fellowship needs.

Reconciling these contradictions makes life rewarding:

* While we accept aloneness in a creative
  sense, we balance it with our fellowship
  needs.

* While we understand that human relations
  are not perfect, we cherish a few vital
  kindred—soul—companionships.

Our kindred soul may be a mate, a lover, friend or relative. It is someone who deserves trust and whose opinions we respect. We are assured of his good will and the abilities to be critical and firm when needed... or to give comforting support. Our kindred soul is motivated by a charitable frame of mind — he wishes to protect us from undue stress... preventing us from magnifying trauma whenever we rationalize. Our friend helps us to get in touch with the better self. And we, the receivers of such gift, are ready to offer the same healing love from the depth of the heart.

POSITIVE CHOICES

We do not always have the choice of sharing life with someone we love passionately. But it is vital to cultivate a kindred—soul—relationship, exchanging emotional intimacy and support. Loneliness teaches us to love in a more rewarding manner — it reveals to us the beauty and fulfillment of its opposite... which is sharing.

CROSSROADS

THE PREMISE:

> Let us become dedicated self-improvers and gently, but firmly regulate the pendulum of choice. Let us use duality to our advantage — turning weakness into strength and replacing fear with confidence, that we may build our happiness in wisdom.

THE REACTIONS:

PESSIMIST:	I don't believe it.
DEFEATIST:	I can't do it.
RATIONALIZER:	It's too much work.
SELF-DOUBTER:	I wish I could try.
SELF-IMPROVER:	Why not? I can master my life.

Americans have reached the cross-roads of choices; we know where we came from, but we have to make up our minds if we like the path ahead. Duality— the old puritan dream versus the temptations of materialism — has left its marks on the life-style of the nation. Could it be that we are entering a new decade of enlightenment?

In the 1970s, perceptions were revised and enlarged by dedicated professionals who opened new frontiers of rationality. We observed the propositions to marry economy to a humanism based on such time-honored concepts as morals and values and the virtues of self-reliance. The bigger-is-better maxim, to which the country is dedicated, was questioned by the small-is-beautiful proponents. In another startling reversal of thinking, the attempt was made to relate modern physics to ancient mystical teachings. Doctors and psychiatrists have observed phenomena and gathered data that would no longer preclude the possibility of the human spirit's survival of death. And increasingly, man's dual physical-spiritual nature is researched from a holistic perspective, with various fields of science uniting for a better understanding. Such trends go beyond the concept of curing ills through ever-expanding technology – they aim to harmonize the modern progress with the wisdom of the ages.

As individuals, we are confronted with the identical task— to master and transcend the worries of our material existence that we may open our minds to loftier concerns. The pendulum of choice swings from chance to purpose, and from error to truth that we may experience the whole of life. It remains our destiny to apply our problem-solving knowledge to the challenges of this world – but we may use our own free will to seek the sanctuary of joy and contentment. What can we achieve in the allotted span of time that we partake and share on earth? We can attempt no more than to creatively enhance the seasons of our lives —to find a meaning that abides within each person's heart .

Index

MEET THE AUTHOR

Johanna Alemann had her early articles published even before she completed her journalistic studies at the universities in Berlin and Prague, and never lost her devotion to chronicling the human condition. Branching out from a rewarding writing career to film-making, she produced her first documentary and upon its critical acclaim, worked as an educational producer-distributor in Los Angeles. She successfully directed her own company for many years, earning a reputation as writer-producer of high-quality standards. Specializing in the humanities, her film series were acquired by schools, universities and libraries throughout the U.S., and in many other parts of the world; they also earned her a wealth of complimentary reviews and over thirty national and international awards.